Rich Hall has written for the American TV shows *Saturday Night Live* and *David Letterman*, for which he won an Emmy. His previous books are *Sniglets* and *Self Help for the Bleak*. When not being pummelled in the ring by light heavyweight boxers, he resides in London and, occasionally, Montana.

things snowball

rich hall

An *Abacus* Book

First published in Great Britain by Abacus in 2002

Copyright © Rich Hall, 2002

The moral right of the author has been asserted.

A number of pieces in this book appeared, in rawer form, in *The Scotsman* ('Portrait of a Head Distressed', 'Great Jokes Squandered', 'Go Home and Practise', 'Stabby Bits', 'Gumball Minutes', 'The Thithterton', 'Birth of the Spatula'), *GQ* ('Where I Hang My Head') and the *Guardian* ('Wrong Way To Heaven').

Lyrics from 'Things Snowball' © John Wesley Harding and Peter Case printed with kind permission of Bug Music BMI/Plangent Visions Music Ltd

Lyrics from 'I'm Not From Here' © James McMurtry printed with kind permission of Bug Music BMI

A CIP catalogue record for this book is available from the British Library.

ISBN 0 349 11510 9

Typeset in Times New Roman by
Palimpsest Book Production Limited,
Polmont, Stirlingshire

Printed and bound in Great Britain by
Clays Ltd, St Ives plc

Abacus
A division of
Time Warner Books UK
Brettenham House
Lancaster Place
London WC2E 7EN

To Kyalika

I was living free up the stairs from a mortuary
He could hear me bring the bodies home at night

'Things Snowball', John Wesley Harding and Peter Case

contents

things snowball

crickets

BACK WHEN I was a kid my grandfolks, who lived in Eastern Tennessee, owned and operated a small nuclear plant – nothing fancy, mind you, just a little 'mom and pop'-type operation, featuring one of those old-fashioned uranium-rod reactors you hardly see anymore and a little cooling-tower, which Granpa painted a cheery blue and yellow. He sold the power to folks in the local community, and not always for money. Sometimes he'd barter.

Granma would sit in the back room – one of two that formed the living quarters – knitting tea cozies and chattering with the customers, who would amble in to pay their bill and end up gossiping away the afternoon. 'She's only gonna stay with him till the kids are grown.' That sort of stuff.

Granpa was a hale, blustery man. He reminded you of Lee Marvin, if Lee Marvin were, say, about 140 pounds heavier and had red curly hair instead of white, and wore glasses. Otherwise a dead ringer. He spent his days loading uranium rods into the reactor, polishing the turbines, or just whiling away the afternoon, gazing out the small window of his control room (panelled in cedar – to me the most delicious, nose-tickling aroma), daydreaming, as he most always did, of fishing. Granpa only seemed to be truly happy when he had traded a U-rod for a fishing rod, a trusty fibreglass Shakespear that seemed to divine vigour from the lake, like a blood trans-fusion. The afternoons we spent fishing together, sitting under a tree, watching enormous, goo-goo-eyed lake trout make lazy circles in the pools of effluent from the core heat-exchanger just downstream from the plant – those are memories no one can take from me. 'You can never catch too many trout!' old Granpa would cackle, sliding another of those fat, phosphorescent beauties off his lure and plopping it into his creel. 'You just can't!'

In June of 1960, when I turned six, I went to stay with Granma and Granpa for the summer. My parents didn't have a lot of money and my dad was pretty despondent most of the time. Mom explained to me it was because he had come to the slow realisation that 'swirling', 'whirling' and 'twirling' were, ultimately, three words that pretty much meant the same thing. Mom said that was depressing him. But I suspect there was more to it than that.

As for staying with Granma and Granpa, I couldn't have been more ecstatic. Granpa pretty much let me have the run of the plant. He gave me little assignments. My favourite was hunting crickets with his 'cricket-finder'. (Later, of course, I would come to know it as a Geiger Counter.) I know Granpa was just being gracious, but I took my little detail very seriously, checking every square inch of the old place. Once, the little machine actually 'found' a cricket. 'Scriddup . . . scriddup . . . scriddup' it chirped, furiously.

It was near a cluster of heat-exchangers. I mentioned it to Granpa that evening at dinner, but instead of locating the insect, Granpa made Granma and me strip naked, and then he threw us together in a cold shower, which made Granma scream. After that he forced us down on the floor and scoured our entire bodies with a metal scrub-brush – not much fun. Granma's blood pressure went way up. The next day some humourless types from the NRC (Nuclear Regulatory Commission) showed up, and made Granpa fill out lots of forms and he got all frazzled and went off fishing. Since then, I've never been that fond of crickets.

That summer, Granma took it upon herself to instil in me a sense of responsibility. I think she felt my parents weren't parenting me very well. One day, when the fish were biting like crazy and Granpa was looking pretty wistful, Granma convinced him to let me take over the reactor.

'It's time the little snapper learned some maturity,' she said.

Granpa stopped loading rods into the reactor. He lifted off his protective lead-lined head cover and studied me quizzically, as if perhaps seeing me in a new perspective.

'Well, little man,' he said. (He'd never called me that before.) 'Think you can keep your eye on this thing?'

'Sure,' I replied, chuffed. I'd seen the process a million times. You just slipped the U-rods into the graphite block thingamajig and lowered it into the 'heavy-water' doohickey, and something and something. Piece of cake. Granpa was already out of his lead suit, and halfway into his waders. He knelt and put a big, red, raw hand on my shoulder.

'Always remember,' he said – and here he was fairly stern – 'you can never put too many rods in the reactor. You just can't!!'

With that, he was out the door. Shortly afterwards Granma went off to town in the big white Buick to run some errands. I looked around the plant, feeling, for the first time in my life, vital. Not just a kid. I wasn't really sure what to do next. I considered throwing a couple of rods into the reactor, the way I'd seen Granpa do. Instead, I climbed into the protective suit, which took about an hour. It was way too big, the squarish head-cover bobbling on my shoulders. The legs bunched up at my ankles, ridiculously. I looked like a walking accordion. It was hot inside there. And foggy. Also, I was beginning to wish Granpa had given me a little more detailed instruction on how to handle a nuclear reactor.

'You can never put too many rods in the reactor,' he had said. 'You just can't!!' Was that an admonishment, meaning, 'you can't put too many rods in the reactor, because it will blow up'? Or had he meant – like the trout – 'no matter how many rods you put in the reactor, you can't put in too many'?

I looked down at the pile of rods on the floor and pondered my dilemma. They didn't look particularly sinister or dangerous to me. They just looked like rods. If I put them all in the reactor, Granpa might be proud of me for my industriousness. On the other hand, if I didn't put *any* in, he might be just as proud of me for my thriftiness. This 'responsibility' business was getting a little tricky. I sat down on the pile of rods to have a good, frustrating cry.

Then, wouldn't you know it, I heard a cricket.

'Scriddup . . . scriddup,' it went. Coming from somewhere under the pile of rods.

Right away, I knew this was trouble. I had to find it and get rid of it before Granpa got back. I sure didn't want to go through that cold shower/wire brush business again! I lifted up one of the rods just in time to glimpse

4

it, black and crackly legged, scuttling further underneath the pile. I lifted up some more rods, set them down behind me, still couldn't find the thing.

'Scriddup . . . scriddup . . .'

I displaced more rods from the pile. Pretty soon I had a whole new stack behind me, but I could still hear that infernal 'scriddup . . . scriddup' coming from the original pile. Finally I was down to one rod. I could hear him under there, clattering away – a bit warily, it seemed to me. Triumphantly, I lifted up the last rod, poised to crush him with my shoe, but the damned protective suit was so clumsy and unwieldy I couldn't really see to get a good stomp on him, and he popped over my foot and resumed his stupid chirping from beneath the new pile.

That was it. I just threw all the rods, one by one, into the reactor, forcing a showdown between the two of us. When the last rod went in, exposing the little bastard for once and all, he sure as hell shut up, perhaps knowing his withering and exquisitely squishy demise was now imminent . . .

Then the reactor core melted down and all hell broke loose in the valley.

Granma and Granpa have been gone quite a while now. And you don't see those old 'mom and pop'-type nuclear plants much anymore. But I think most of us probably have an idea of the exact moment in our lives when we realised what the word 'responsibility' really means. I sure learned what it meant that summer. ('He's the one *responsible*!!' – how many times did I hear *that* from the locals? Not to mention the NRC.) And for that I have my grandfolks to thank. Granpa, wherever you are, I hope you're catching the big trout.

portrait of a head
distressed

I T IS THE Haircut That Made Time Stand Still. It defies style or description. It is an obscenity, a fiasco, a felony. The man who perpetrated it should be wrapped in concertina wire, and gaffer-taped to a wild bronco. He should be shackled to a stake and consumed by dung beetles. Why he is allowed to live, to continue his heinous butchering, while I slink the streets and children recoil in horror, dogs bury their heads, whimpering at the pure inhumanity of what they have witnessed, is beyond mortal comprehension. Grown men see me, turn fish-faced and weep openly. The horrors of famine and pestilence are chump change compared to my head – a shapeless and indefinable follicular abortion. It is a crime against nature.

A million pounds to the poet who can convincingly describe what's been done to the top of my head! Another million to the physicist who can explain how my current haircut can defy gravity and physical form as we know it. It disproves everything Isaac Newton laboured to prove in his lifetime. In a mere twenty minutes some fuckwit with a pair of shears – whose name I've chosen to forget, whose face I've burned from memory, though I'm sure it's featured somewhere in the painting of *Dante's Inferno*, cackling, mincing maniacally beneath a sign that reads 'Walk-Ins Welcome' at the entrance to Hell – has managed to transform my slightly overgrown but otherwise passable head of hair into something I can only describe as a coxcomb of freshly chucked-up cat hairballs lying atop a patch of dead swamp sawgrass, bordered by a pair of hirsute croissants that recall to mind Princess Leia from *Star Wars*, if someone had dunked her head in one of those pneumatic aeroplane toilets and given it a good flush. This is only a temporal description, for even as I write this the haircut, to my astonishment, seems to be mutating. A drop in barometric pressure changes it to the shape and consistency of milk-withered Weetabix. The wind comes up and, amazingly, it becomes a Hydra of steel wool and cacti branches. This very morning I dislodged from it a small tit-mouse, who apparently believed my hair to be natural habitat. Someone remarked, after it was briefly rained on, that it wasn't a haircut at all but rather 'a kelp exhibit that had lost its funding'. Chemotherapy patients have been sending me sympathy cards.

Perhaps I deserve it. I live in a town where all haircuts seem like an afterthought. There are women in my town with mullets who aren't even lesbians. (Some even have two mullets. Don't ask me to explain.) Perhaps I shouldn't have entrusted my personal grooming to a stranger, a mountebank, a tonsillatory cutpurse who for all I know has been on a three-day methamphetamine binge and simply wandered into the salon, donned an apron and attempted to pass himself off as a barber. Federal monitoring of this particular occupation should be mandatory: I am now a walking testament to that. Fighting, I understand, has temporarily stopped in Palestine. They have set down their guns and offered up a Day of Condolence in sympathy to me. The United Nations has dipped into its World Relief Fund to provide 'suitable shelter and cover' for my head. Pakistan and India have abandoned their nuclear weapons development. 'We have now seen the Horror and Devastation one human can perpetrate upon another and we are truly remorseful,' said Pakistan's President Pervez Musharraf. 'Thank God we didn't have to witness it first-hand,' added North Korea's President Kim Chong-il. Asked to comment, Prime Minister Blair was quoted as saying, 'After seeing Rich Hall's head, I think we all owe Michael Bolton an apology.'

'Don't worry, it'll grow out,' say my friends, even as the frozen horror and astonishment on their faces betray their cheap placation. That's like telling the mother of the young Elephant Man that her kid would 'grow out of it'. My hair will grow out the way kudzu grows out. It will grow like stalactites, like a topiary garden groomed by a chimp. Children will get lost in it and go slowly insane. It will feature as the subject of a Stephen King novel. It will grow out with bald spots that follow you around the room like the eyes of Jesus in one of those creepy Tijuana souvenir wall hangings. It will give people the 'willies' and the 'heebie-jeebies'.

What can you learn from my experience? Keep a hawk's wary eye on the man or woman who wields the scissors; question every snip. They get to go home absolved: you have to live with the freshly butchered

9

the phineas gage
letters
(1848–1849)

F EW CASES IN abnormal psychology are as compelling
as that of Phineas Gage. In 1848 Gage, a foreman
for the Rutland & Burlington (Vermont) Railroad, was
clearing a railway path when an accidental explosion sent
a crowbar flying through his head. Amazingly, he
appeared unaffected by the incident. (In fact, after a quick
visit to a nearby doctor, he went back to work.)
Subsequently, he was evaluated by a handful of doctors
who concluded that the only significant change in Gage's
behaviour was that he had become more 'irritable'. The
following letters, only recently made public, were penned
to his wife over a period of several months following the
incident. Personally, I believe they provide some insight
into the testiness of Gage's nature.

Dearest Darling Ida,

I hope this letter finds you well. I miss you, and think of you constantly. Work is going well. We have laid over twelve miles of track in the last two weeks. The weather here is quite spectacular. The trees are turning a lustrous yellow, and there is the sweet tantalizing smell of sugar maple in the air, though not as tantalizing as your fragrance, dear, which I miss so, so much.

Not much news here to speak of. We have a new track foreman named O'Brien, an Irishman. Saturday, we reached a village called Cavendish, and the following morning I attended the local service. The Reverend talked about the glory of redemption and how we all need to be grateful for the wonderful things the Lord has provided us. Later we pitched horseshoes and Injun' Joe and I threw double ringers. Also, yesterday a two-and-a-half-foot length of crowbar accidentally passed through my skull and landed about fifty yards away. Can't think of much else that's happened. Give my love to your folks. Write soon.

      Your loving husband,
      Phineas

                      November 25

Dearest Darling Ida,

How delightful to hear from you. Even though you chastise me for my tardiness in replying to your previous letter, I do miss you and apologise for my delay in writing. I meant to post this letter sooner, but it slipped my mind. I suppose there are two reasons for this.

Firstly, we have been very busy clearing the Montpelier–Rutland stretch, which is almost entirely comprised of bedrock and has proved to be quite resistant to track-laying.

Secondly. I don't know if I mentioned this before but a crowbar passed through my head.

Still, you remain my true and precious love.

Your loving husband,
Phineas

December 30

Dear.

You have expressed disappointment in my not returning for Christmas, although I was certainly there with you in my thoughts, or rather, those thoughts which weren't obliterated by the CROWBAR WHICH PASSED THROUGH MY HEAD several months ago. I trust you all had a wonderful and glorious day. I can imagine the smell of the turkey and trimmings. In fact imagining smells is pretty much all I do, ever since A CROWBAR PASSED THROUGH MY HEAD.

As for my own Christmas day, I spent the bulk of it resting and trying to be grateful for all the miracles God has bestowed upon me. The birth of the saviour Jesus, for instance: a constant miracle. As well, the bountifulness of this great and vast land and its offerings – that too is a miracle. The great cycle of life and death and life renewed again – truly that is a miracle. I trust that you share this wonderment with me, and never forget that we are here by the grace of God only. By the way, it suddenly occurred to me that another miracle would be the fact that

13

I'm even able to write this letter to you, considering . . . and I can't stress this enough . . . A CROWBAR PASSED THROUGH MY HEAD. Therefore, perhaps you can find it in your heart to stop bitching and moaning about my not being home for Christmas. I meant to, but wasn't quite up to the fifteen-hundred-mile rail journey. One guess as to why.

> The usual niceties,
> Phineas

January 7

Dearest what'syourname,

You're right. I did forget your mother's birthday. In fact, I'll go so far as to say I've forgotten your mother's name. And your father's. Also, yours.

   Let me offer this suggestion for my apparent gaffe. It is within the realm of plausibilty that maybe . . . just maybe . . . and I realise I'm going out on a limb here . . . but there is ever-so-slight a possibility that the reason I forgot your mother's birthday owes something to the fact that **A CROWBAR PASSED THROUGH MY HEAD!**

> But then again, I'm no doctor.
> Cheers,
> Phineas

hot august meal

NEIL DIAMOND CALLED me last week. Right out of the blue.

'I'm a fan,' he said. 'Come over and let me make you some dinner.' Inexplicably, he added, 'And wear a safety helmet of some kind.'

I accepted the invitation. As for the remark about the helmet, I just figured ol' Neil was having some renovation done on his home and had my safety in mind. It was flattering to be invited to Casa Diamond, though I have to say, I haven't even thought about Neil Diamond in five or six years, much less purchased any of his cds. In fact, I often confuse Neil Diamond with some okra. They're both slithery and often undercooked.

Anyway, here's me pulling up to Neil's gated mansion, thinking to myself, 'Man o' man, you just never know what kinda curve life is gonna throw you. Dinner with Neil Diamond!' Neil lives in one of those very exclusive Bel Air neighbourhoods. However, you can buy a map to his home from any of those hawkers on Sunset Boulevard. Sometimes Neil himself likes to stand out there in the hot, blistering sun, selling maps to his own home. He's that kind of guy. But he wasn't out there on Sunset Boulevard today. Nope. He was in his kitchen, making me – Rich Hall – dinner.

A low hydraulic 'whoosh', unseen, ushered me through the Diamond compound's delicately filigreed wrought iron gates, and I cruised up a winding, lushly overgrown driveway adorned with ferns, hibiscus and hydrangeas. I noted, with some detachment, that they were all growing out of discarded KFC buckets. That's Neil, ever the conscientious recycler. I looked around for any building work going on, but there didn't seem to be any. I felt a little dumb, wearing a hardhat.

Neil greeted me at the door. The man hasn't changed all that much from his Hot August Night days. He still has a leonine mane of hair, particularly if the dictionary you own happens to define 'leonine' as 'looking like someone glued bits of sock fluff to a light bulb'. He was decked out in a rhinestone-studded denim suit and cowboy boots, and had a slight paunch, which teasingly obscured a big customised belt buckle that spelled out, I believe, 'SWANKY BOY'. He was cradling what appeared to be an infant against his shoulder. It was swaddled in a fleecy pink blanket and I was moved by Neil's paternal posture. As he introduced himself I attempted to get a glimpse of the baby, but Neil was cooing and cradling it very protectively.

An awkward question passed through my head. Was it Neil's child or grandchild? I didn't want to insult Neil, right from the get-go, by suggesting incumbent grandparentage, if, in fact, he was a proud and virile father. You know these showbiz types: they can procreate quite

16

ripely and nobody is ever surprised. The question quickly dissipated, however, when I finally got a good look, and realised Neil was actually cradling nothing more than a large, unboiled prawn in a toddler's blanket. Had I known him more familiarly, I probably would have made a casual inquiry, something along the lines of, 'Hey, Neil, how come you're cuddling a prawn?' But I let it pass.

'That's a nice hardhat you're wearing, friend,' remarked Neil in that same low, dusky voice that made so many of us swoon when he used to intro 'I Am, I Said'. He eyed it and whistled appreciatively. I'd only just purchased it at a builders supply shop on the way to Bel Air. In fact, Neil seemed downright animated, to the extent where I felt obliged to remove it and present it to him for perusal.

Gently setting the prawn down on the fat, expensive foyer carpet, he took the helmet into his hands and admired its contours.

'Whew . . .' he gurgled. 'Adjustable brow support. Very high quality. Very nice. Is it OSHA approved?' (OSHA stands for Occupational Safety and Health Administration, a watchdog arm of the US Government.)

'Uh, yeah, sure, Neil. I guess it is,' I replied. He replaced it gingerly atop my head. At this point, I was starting to feel a bit weird.

Neil led me into his massive living room, which was handsomely decorated – a testimony to a man well cultured and fêted by the world. There were leopard prints on the furniture, Ming Dynasty urns, gold records on the wall, sterling silver ensconced photos of Neil gyrating on the world's great stages. Above a daunting river rock fireplace, big enough to walk inside, hung a life-sized oil portrait of Neil looking stalwart and noble. On his head was a yellow hardhat.

Over roast duck and port, Neil took me into his

confidence. You'd have thought he'd known me for ages. He was tremendously excited about a film project he had in development: an epic biopic of Latrell Sprewell. Neil was going to write the script, score the music, play the eponymous role, produce – the whole deal. He was so enthusiastic about the project it became a slightly delicate problem for me to ask who, exactly, Latrell Sprewell was.

'Power forward for the New York Knicks,' Neil replied, matter of factly. 'Big black man. Quick as lightning. And a killer three-point-shooter.'

I don't recall much of what happened after that. The port kept flowing hard and heavy, Neil got out his guitar and launched into a medley serenade, and somewhere around 'Song Sung Blue' I passed out. When I awoke, it must have been the middle of the night. I was lying on a couch. Neil was kind of hovering over me, predatorily.

'I want that hardhat,' he said, but his voice was whispery and quite sinister. Something snapped in me. This wasn't the Neil Diamond who had made so many of us sing blithely along to 'Sweet Caroline'. This was Neil Diamond, hardhat frottager. I shot out of that mansion like a rocket, into the safety of the Bel Air night. The helmet flew off somewhere in Neil's living room, and I felt a sickening squish beneath my feet as I was barrelling through the foyer. I remember thinking, 'My god, my god, I've killed Neil Diamond's precious prawn,' but brother, I didn't look back.

Then yesterday, as I was driving along a non-descript street in one of LA's industrial neighbourhoods, what do I come across but a grand-opening display for Neil Diamond's World of Hardhats. That's when I put two and two together. Neil must think no one is going to make the connection between Neil Diamond, world famous singing sensation and some guy named Neil Diamond who steals people's personal safety equipment then tries to pass it off as *new*! He presumes people will drive by, see the name on the building and think to themselves, 'Nah, it can't be *that* Neil Diamond.' Well, I'm here to tell you, my friend, it is. Deal with it!

How many unsuspecting victims like myself have been lured into this man's scam?

If anyone else has had a similar experience, please contact me through the publishers. I always told myself that if I ever wrote a book I wouldn't use it as a bully pulpit or to wring revenge against people who have gotten on my bad side. But I feel duped and betrayed by someone I grew up admiring. So thanks a lot, Neil, thanks for ruining a dream.

waltzing the ladder

I NEEDED A LADDER to reach the light fixtures in my house. It was my annual clean-the-dead-flies-out-of-the-globes detail, which usually takes place in October. In Montana, this signals the arrival of what we call winter, and what the rest of the world would call The Abbreviated Glacial Age. Flies in Montana choose to fry themselves to death rather than endure the oncoming deep freeze.

Since I didn't own a ladder, I trotted down to Peplo's Hardware to peruse their selection. I might as well have been purchasing a handgun. They made me fill out safety forms, mailing lists and warranty vouchers. A ladder, as far as I know, is a simple, primitive device. Millions of people throughout history have used them, with little or no instruction. But apparently a few lost souls haven't quite grasped the fundamentals, because now ladders come with a detailed list of instructions. Personally, I'd always assumed ladder operation was fairly straight-forward:

1.   Set up ladder
2.   Ascend it
3.   Come back down

Wrongo. My five-step ladder offers no less than *twenty-three* steps of instruction. They're printed right there on the side, underneath a hieroglyph of a stickman falling to what looks like an untimely, horrific death from a height of roughly two and a half feet.

Out of curiosity I called my neighbour, Norbert, who used to be employed by the North American Strategic Command, which monitors America's missile silos. Norbert informed me there were only six steps for operating a nuclear warhead, which not only gives you an idea of how overly cautious these ladder manufacturers are, but also the kind of people I have for neighbours.

The very first point of ladder instruction is, quite rightly, the sagest:

DO NOT USE LADDER IF YOU TIRE EASILY

Hmmmm. Seems to me that's probably a crackerjack good reason for *using a ladder in the first place*. Hanging from light fixtures by my fingertips was, frankly, wearing me out. Apparently ladders are only for the peppy and the vigorous. This same instruction goes on to warn against using the ladder 'if you are using medicine or alcohol', which is disappointing, considering how often I enjoy quaffing six or seven pints before popping into the toolshed for some joy-climbing.

DO NOT 'WALK' OR 'JOG' YOUR LADDER

I'm not making this up. Obviously some people are confusing their ladders with dogs or personal fitness trainers.

I believe what they mean is: it's not a good idea to pogo your ladder over to a new spot on the floor. It's interesting, however, to see that these Ladder Abuse Researchers have actually designated two official speeds, 'walk' and 'jog', for this particular form of amusement.

DO NOT USE LADDER AS A SHELF

Hell. No wonder all my Fabergé Eggs fell off and shattered.

STORE IN A SAFE, DRY PLACE

This instruction always kills me, as it is the most superfluous advice for humans since TRY TO REMEMBER TO BREATHE. 'Store in a safe, dry place' applies to pretty much everything that exists in our known world. It explains why we don't keep cheese in the bathtub. Food, tools, appliances, medicine, fertilisers, currency, solvents, pants, my neighbour's nuclear devices . . . all should be kept in safe, dry places. Even deodorant, which is made for wet, funky places, explicitly requests to be 'kept in a safe, dry place'.

Step nine is somewhat frightening:

FACE LADDER WHEN CLIMBING. KEEP BODY CENTRED BETWEEN SIDE RAILS. DO NOT ALLOW MORE THAN ONE PERSON AT A TIME ON LADDER.

I can't imagine the grisly tableau that warranted this admonishment. Maybe a set of dyslexic Siamese-Triplet housepainters plunged several feet to their death. C'mon, it's a ladder for chrissake. There's one way up and one way down. Whether you land on your feet or your cranium is proportionate to your level of stupidity, right?

America is the most litigious nation on earth. People will catch their genitals in zips, then sue the trouser manufacturers. (Hence, 'to sue the pants off someone'.) We have created an entire industry of personal liability watchdogs and idiot advisory boards. The bottom of my ladder's instruction label has a 24-hour toll-free number for 'questions on your ladder'. Somewhere, some hapless person is sitting by a phone, waiting for some dillweed to call them up at three a.m.:

'Is it okay to take my ladder out waltzing?'

The answer is 'no'. It might injure itself and sue you.

merman

AS A COLLECTOR of vintage comic books, I have been trying to locate any avid followers of the somewhat hapless Superheroes listed below. Neither of these characters really caught on, essentially due to clerical errors. Looking back, I can understand why. I suppose most readers weren't ready for them.

One was MerMan. MerMan – ordained by the Hero High Command as Protector of the Deep – was half-human, half-fish. He possessed astonishing swim skills and could communicate with fish and other sea creatures. He was equally at home on dry land, though here his super-powers were fairly moot. He had to get around in a wheel-chair. Because of the fins.

During MerMan's Sacred Ritual of Ordainment, Morpheus, the Bestower of Powers, who was getting on a bit, mispronounced MerMan's name, so that it came out rhyming with 'German' or 'vermin'. Because nothing uttered during the Sacred Ritual could be recanted,

MerMan (now Merman) effectively became the first and only ever Jewish Superhero.

Normally, this shouldn't have been a problem, but as an essential Do-Gooder, Merman became increasingly appalled by what he saw as a growing onslaught of Pure Evil in the world. This prompted his spiritual retreat into Orthodox Judaism. Consequently he refused to fight crime on the Sabbath. His arch-enemies simply waited until Saturday to ply their evil. Fairly heady stuff for a comic book.

Merman's crime-fighting partner was Incest Boy. With his overdeveloped thorax and ability to carry twenty times his own weight, Incest Boy was *supposed* to be 'Insect Boy' – Vanguard of the Insect Kingdom. Unfortunately (again due to the dyslexic bungling of Morpheus), Incest Boy could only summon his Superhuman Buglike Powers after poking his sister. As you can well imagine, amongst a legion of rigidly moral and righteous Superheroes, Incest Boy was more or less confined to society's margins.

The two appeared together in a series of comic books in the sixties. If anyone remembers them or owns back issues, I would love to hear from you. Below are some letters I recently unearthed in my parents' attic, which were returned to me, unanswered, by a certain Mr Hoopley, the editor of Merman/Incest Boy comics. I include them in the hope they may jog your memory. Bear in mind I was only nine when I wrote them.

Dear Mr Hoopley,

I enjoyed with keen interest your issue #3. But as a careful reader I have a bone to pick with you. Here it is:

On page 4, when Merman is waiting for the

bus to take him downtown to talk to the Harbor City Police Chief about the outbreak of radio-active crab lice, he spots The Crabster across the street in a pet shop. Merman confronts him and a confrontation occurs. Good fight scene. But since he's The Crabster, he moves side-ways, whereas Merman is in his wheelchair and can only move back and forth, so wouldn't The Crabster actually of gotten away?

In my creative writing class, Mr Doughtery stresses that you have to pay attention to detail. I feel you have made an oversite in this regard.

Other than that, I think it was a terrific issue, but how about more illustrations of Incest Boy 'doing it' with his sister, please! Those are my favorite parts.

Yours,
Rich H.

Dear Mr Hoopley,

Fantastic issue #5!! Consider me your number one fan. The Sis Fiddler and his Bottom Feeding Buddy are definitely the best Evilfighters ever! Question: What state is Harbor City located in? My mom says that incest is illegal in most states and that Incest Boy would be thrown in jail for 'doing it' with his sister. Mom, it's a comic book, I told her! Superman would be arested for flying without a license in the real world! That's why they're called Superheroes. She needs to lighten up.

Incest Boys alter ego is mild mannered larva collector N.T. Mollogy. Technically, if *he* were to 'do it' with Incest Boys sister, would that be considered incest as well? And would it be illegal?

I thought the storyline where Incest Boy drags the Lost City of Atlantis across the International Date line so Merman can resume fighting the Aqualords was enspired. My mom said that Merman was probably a sturgeon or lox. Then she laughed. What's so funny about that?

Keep up the good work,
Rich H.

Dear Mr Hoopley,

Please, please, please print my letter! I want all my friends to know that I am your most faithful fan. We all think I-Boy and the Mermster kick butt. When they were hanging from giant fish hooks as whale bait because the Lobster Pot Poachers wanted them out of the way . . . enspired. Also, the stuff about Merman consoling Incest Boy over his 'guilt' was very imformative. He's right (Merman). There are some things we have no control over. In creative writing class we have discussed character flaws. Our teacher lectured to us about Oedippus (spelling?) and some bells went off – not the class bell, ha, ha, bells of recognition. All good characters have to be messed up some way and I think those are what make Merman and Incest Boy unique. 'What doesn't kill us makes us stronger.' That's what my teacher says.

Humbly and faithfully,
Rich H.
PS please print this

Dear Mr Hoopley,

If Incest Boy derives his strength from 'doin' it'
with his sister, would he get at least a 'buzz'
from, say, a cousin?

       Just asking,
       Rich H.

Mr Hoopley,

How come you never print any of my letters?

       Why?
       Rich H.

aberdeen like

A BERDEEN. FANTASTIC TOWN!
The nightlife teems like no other. As an example, go to 12 Bridge Street, right next to the Sta-Fluff Dry Cleaners, knock on the brown door and ask for 'Irvine'. Bring your own nibbles. On my last visit to this cracklin' city (and I visit often), the people were in a particularly festive mood. McDonald's had just introduced a new tartar sauce to its Filet-O-Fish sandwich – with 'a lot more pickle'. I got in on the tail end of the celebration. There's nothing better than experiencing a town when it's feeling really good about itself.

If you're visiting for the first time, allow me to offer you my customised walking tour. I think you'll find it invigorating.

From the railway station, turn left. Look for a big, grey, foreboding mass of oppressive and squarish granite with some tiny windows. You'll recognise this as the City of Aberdeen. Now get back on the train. Quickly.

Just kidding. Cross the street, being careful to watch out for displaced Texans, with steer longhorns attached to the bonnets of their Fiat Puntos, driving on the wrong side of the road. There's oil money in Aberdeen, lots of it. (A lot of the party action in Aberdeen is offshore.)

Walk about three hundred metres and you'll find yourself in the heart of Aberdeen's bustling shopping district, called Poundstretchers. Sample the delights. Keep an eye out for one of the many kiosks where matronly Scotswomen sell the local delicacy: batter-fried chunks of granite.

Across from Poundstretchers is the inspirational war memorial – a massive granite carving of some soldiers resting against a handsome slab of granite. Inscribed in relief are the words:

In Memory of the Valiant Men and Women of World War II, who Gave Their Lives in the Cause of Freedom Like

Strange verbiage there but, like I said, quite inspiring and reverential.

Cross the road in front of the Memorial and you will arrive at the Aberdeen Art Gallery. On my last several visits it has been offering a wonderfully minimalist exhibition of hand-painted 'Closed' signs.

From the Gallery, you have two options. You can continue left past the University and then uphill to Mounthooley, which takes you to Old Town. Or you can stand right where you are and pray for a huge chunk of granite to fall from a building on to your head and put you out of your misery.

Should you choose to continue living, you will soon find yourself in the lively University area. The University of Aberdeen is at the forefront of Aerodynamic Research, notably evident by the number of flying-saucer-shaped research material being sailed around the commons.

Continue across the campus and you will notice two small edifices in front of the dining complex, which appear to be either minarets or a pair of large chess bishops which have been pebble-dashed and glazed in creosote. If you ask the majority of passersby what they are, they will likely tell you they're 'Dunnaes'. My research revealed the minarets are a tribute to Aberdeen's most famous poet, Elphin Cruickshank, who in 1560 penned the Immortal *Ode to an Unmarried Daughter*:

> Ooh supple mistress, ye
> hair like straw hangin' oot a couch
> bile your heid o' sweet missus, ouch
> slabberchops at your feet
> pestilence and dribble
> hing aboot, hing aboot
> and nary a clappydoo tae feed them
> like

Cruickshank is much loved and oft quoted in Aberdeen. Many of his poetic phrases are part of the everyday lingo. Two I overheard a lot were, 'Oot my way ya' dunce!' and, 'I think I drapt some bad e.'

Now down to the docks, a must see. For certainly they are the auricle and ventricle of The Granite City's life-flow. Ships of every nation burgeon within the watery warrens of Aberdeen's harbour. It's a maritime version of the Worlds Fair. Also, the pervading rust is a welcome respite from the predominately grey scheme to which one's eyes have become accustomed. Last I was there, I watched a team of burly, jocular stevedores unload a massive crate of imported Albanians. I could have spent the whole afternoon down there but a frigate bird became carnally fascinated by my metal belt buckle and I had to scurry. Good thing too, because there was so much else to see in town. I can't begin to list it all, but a highlight was a small tot sitting in the doorway of an estate house attempting to smash a 9-volt battery with an axe. His mother appeared in the doorway and gently wrested the battery from his grasp. Scenes like that renew my faith in humankind. Me, I shall always remember Aberdeen.

Ah, for the love of Christ. I gotta apologise. I don't know what's gotten into me. For the three previous pages I've unfairly and mercilessly trashed the city of Aberdeen. Yes, Scotland, your Aberdeen – your gleaming granite Citadel. What was I thinking? How unfair to make fun of a town just because it consists primarily of rock. Is geology not above reproach? It was a cheap shot. Aberdeen is not grey and oppressive. It is sturdy and massive. It is Scotland's right shoulder – the one you can always lean on. (Scotland's left shoulder, incidentally, is the Western Isles – equally as lovely but wetter. It's more the shoulder you cry on.)

I'm kicking myself right now, reader. All Aberdeen ever did on my visits there was extend its graciousness to me, and I stabbed it in the back. (Or shoulder, if we're to stick with the aforementioned flimsy metaphor.) The only explanation I can offer for such a vicious diatribe is this: Comedic Pressure.

Writing comedy isn't easy. Most writing, be it books or periodicals, has a purposeful construct – to move the reader, to take the reader through an emotional journey. But comedy writing is different. It's bullshit. That's right. Equal parts bombast and triviality, no matter how its authority is perceived. And if you think it's easy to churn out a lifetime of pointless drivel, think again, friend. I've read *Finnegan's Wake*. I'd love to crank out that kind of made-to-order assignment. But no, I'm the make-me-laugh guy. I gotta bake it from goddamn scratch every time. And what happened was, I was walking around Aberdeen, enjoying the sea breeze, the smiles, the stolid architecture and then, all of a sudden in the back of my head, I get that gnawing, pestering comedy voice in my head, the one that says 'always tear down, never build up . . .' The more I enjoyed my stroll, the guiltier I felt. Guilt turned to anger and I turned on Aberdeen.

I could've sat down at my typewriter and written about how lovely the city was, but that would make me a travel writer and travel writers are whores. Give them a free meal and a cozy bed and they'll glow about it for two thousand words. It wouldn't matter if it was the Guts of Hell.

Chiang Mai prison was delightful! We snuggled up twelve to a straw mat and at breakfast were served a hearty ration of maggoty suet. Highly recommended.

Well, I won't succumb to that kind of cheap logrolling. So I took the comedic route and made fun of Aberdeen, assuming readers can always find succour in the Theatre of Cruelty. It was cheap and easy and once I started I couldn't stop.

So I'm sorry, Aberdeen. I got caught in a downward spiral of nattering negativity. I was under pressure. I wish

my life as a bluesman

I GOTTA RIGHT to sing the Blues. This despite several legal injunctions to prevent me from doing so. Let me tell you something, Mister Man: I was born with the Blues. Came outta my momma's womb like a bolt of blue, screaming blue murder till I was blue in the face, a blue-eyed baby. This, incidentally, during a blue moon. I'm blue now, even as we speak. 100% blue. I'm so blue I look like Mike Tyson punched a smurf. I'm so blue when I go swimming I leave a residue, like Toilet Duck. Chameleons cross the street to avoid me. I think that qualifies me, thank you very much, as a certified Bluesman. Don't let my suburban upbringing fool you.

They say you have to sell your soul to the devil to really play the Blues. This I did, though several days later the Devil returned and tried to give it back.

'I wasn't thinking clearly at the time,' he announced. 'Your soul is worthless.' I pointed out that the transaction, which took place at a crossroads somewhere in

Mississippi (now the site of a brand new Walmart), was binding. He claimed he was entitled to a five-day 'cooling off period'. Fine. If fame has eluded me, there's your reason. My advice to any would-be Bluesman is try to get something in writing from the Devil.

What do we really mean by the term 'Blues'? Here's my description and I think it's pretty accurate: Have you ever gotten up in the middle of a restless night to get a glass of warm milk and slammed your toe on the sharp metal edge of the bedframe? Notice there's a delay of three or four seconds before the crippling, agonising pain actually settles in? Most of us would take advantage of those few seconds of blissful non-feeling to contemplate God's wonderful creations. But it's the person who slams his foot into the bed three or four more times, just to take advantage of those few precious moments of nothingness, who knows the true meaning of the word 'Blues'. Another way would be to look up 'Blues' in the dictionary.

That my songs have never been recorded is due primarily to the interference of the United States Government. In 1948, when Blues music was at the height of its ascendancy, the government instituted a program to rehabilitate Bluesmen, fearing, apparently, that the Blues was leading to a national epidemic of malaise and melancholia. I was summoned to Spudge, Mississippi, to consult with a government-appointed psychotherapist whose name, I recall, was either Mr Spuerling or Mr Smith Kline Beacham – I often get those two names confused. At the time I was Living the Blues pretty much twenty-four hours a day. In fact my clothes were held together with baling wire. I sat in a dank, nondescript office, idly fingering my gut-strung six-string guitar while Mr Spuerling droned off a litany of probing questions.

38

'When you woke up this morning how did you feel?' he began.

I told him I woke up feeling bad. I was a consummate professional.

'Was there anxiety?' he asked, making small notes into a folder. Then he went into a lot of psycho-claptrap about fear, hostility, poverty, stuff like that. He asked me how I really felt about 'havin' no chicken in the pot' and if a 'gubment man like him was making me feel bad'. Frankly, I didn't like where he was going with all of this. I felt he was trying to undermine my creative reserves. So I clammed up and the next thing I knew they had me in a ward of some kind all strung out on sedatives. The whole thing struck me as invasive and slightly insidious. And all I got paid was fifty lousy dollars. Assholes.

A great old Bluesman – I think it was either Slim Chance or Smith Kline Beacham, again, I get those two confused – once said to me, 'son, you ain't known the Blues until a matchbox can hold your clothes.' Unfortunately, because my parents owned closets I wasn't able to claim that particular hardship. I did once attempt to cram my fairly extensive wardrobe into a matchbox but I couldn't get much more in there than a pair of cufflinks. I don't know how these guys do it. My own approach was to try to stretch the lexicon of Blues Music and sort of 'take it into the future' as it were. For example, I was the first Bluesman to incorporate topics like space exploration and chrome-plating techniques into traditional Blues Music. And for this effort I was rewarded with abject and crushing indifference. Still, and I can't say this enough, I gotta right to sing the Blues.

What few can appreciate is that the Blues is truly the most economic form of musical expression. It is this very stern delineation of vocabulary that separates a true Blues song from, say, a police report. One of my most oft-performed songs (though not necessarily oft-requested) was inspired, as all truly great Blues songs are, by an actual event that happened to me back in the mid-seventies. Here's the gist of it.

I had a girlfriend who at the time lived in Madagascar. The international telephone code happens to be 911. Unfortunately, every time I tried to call her the police would show up at my door, responding to a 911 emergency call. Once I made the mistake of answering the door with a freshly grilled pork chop in my hand. One of the policemen mistook the pork chop for a gun and, dropping to one knee, aimed his gun at me and ordered me to 'drop my weapon'. Whilst I was calmly trying to point out to him that the 'weapon' was actually my dinner a car wheeled around the corner and backfired. The officer with the drawn gun mistakenly believed I was shooting at him and fired back . . . The bullet ricocheted off a ceramic garden gnome and penetrated his thigh. The next thing I know I'm in prison. True story.

Now, relating that chain of events within a Blues song takes a bit of judicious wordplay. One has to capture not only the almost Biblical Misfortune of such an event but also invoke sympathy to the sufferer's plight and subsequent grief. My particular genius for just that sort of thing saw the song unfold like this:

> Lord I'm in the slammer
> Lord I'm feelin' so bad
> (repeat 4 times)

See there? Don't tell me I don't have a right to sing the Blues.

To say I'm the most misunderstood Bluesman ever

would be an understatement. And by 'misunderstood' I'm not referring to the shimmering ephemerality of my chord structures or the multi-layered nuances of my lyrics. I literally mean 'misunderstood'. A good example would be my song 'Deathrow Blues', which was recorded by the great Blustery Bill Bottomdollar as well as several lesser known Bluesmen:

> A lonely room is where I sit
> Full of anger and regret
> Wish I could smoke one cigarette
> But no . . . no . . . no . . .
>
> A man in coat and tie of grey
> I hear his footsteps come my way
> Puts his hand on mine to say
> 'Son, it's time to go'
>
> And now I'm takin' that long walk
> to that seat where they strap you in
> I know soon that I'll see
> My dear old mom and dad again
> But we just sit there on the runway
> And we wait till God knows when
> I got those (deathrow) blues again.
>
> (© Copyright Bug Music Inc.)

Stupid, dimwit publishers. The song was supposed to be called 'Heathrow Blues'. I never been on Deathrow in my life.

Still, I gotta right to sing the Blues.

where i hang my head

B Y NOW, I'M sure just about everyone has seen *Trainspotting*. Personally, though I don't have any problems with the realistic depictions of heroin injection, I did find one scene in the movie ridiculously unbelievable. It's the one where Renton goes to London and gets a job as an estate agent, then lets his mates stay at one of his listed properties for free. The reason this scene is implausible is because *no estate agent in London would ever show that much initiative.*

The combined efforts of all the estate agents in Greater London couldn't ruffle the tuft on a Jaybird's ass. They are Cro-Magnons.

A couple of months ago I inherited some money from a passing relative. (It was my uncle Jerome, if you must know. He got killed in an altercation in front of a drive-in theatre projection shack.) I had two choices on how to spend the inheritance. 1) Give 60% of it in taxes to my US Government 2) buy a flat in London or, 3) go back to school and learn how to count.

I settled for option 2. I'm tired of renting these furnished silage pits where the bathroom has hot and cold running waterbugs and the mattress is a primitive attempt to imitate a mattress by pouring aquarium gravel into a bin-liner and rudely covering it in coconut husks. There's a thin line in London between 'To Let' and 'Toilet'.

I walked into an estate agents in London called Tatworths. It featured enticing photos in the window of lustily appointed, reasonably priced flats that didn't really exist – a trick similar to one used by cheesy striptease clubs.

I approached an agent sagging behind a gun-metal grey desk, who regarded me with all the enthusiasm of a Haitian man being told he's won two tickets to a Bernard Manning concert. He was about seventeen and wore an oleaginous-looking suit and a Slipknot souvenir tie. His previous line of employment, I believe, had been fishing trolleys out of the canal that runs behind the local Safeway.

'Can I help you?' he muttered sullenly.

'I'm looking for a flat,' I chirped.

'Have you registered with us?' he said.

This threw me. 'Registered?'

'Yeah, ahh . . . is your financing in order?'

'As a matter of fact it is, you smarmy garden weasel,' I said, as liltingly as possible. 'Say, why don't you look around the room, find somebody with a bigger desk than yours and let me talk to them?'

He disappeared. A nervous, gun-metal-grey-templed guy, who looked like one of the main characters in a panto version of *Glengarry Glen Ross*, emerged. His name turned out to be Harry.

'What exactly are you looking for?' Harry asked, then let his eyes glaze over while I replied.

44

'Just a nice, airy flat – one bedroom – something quiet and functional,' I said.

Obviously, the operative word in that sentence for Harry was 'something'. He made vague arrangements to meet me the following day and assured me he knew of a few things 'right up my alley'.

The first place we looked at was right up an alley. Calling it a crack house would be an insult to the decorating skills of crack addicts. I dismissed it immediately, which is why it's now probably a Nationally Protected Drug Habitat.

'It's been on the market for a while,' Harry said helpfully. 'You could probably make a low offer.'

'Whew! They warned me about your high-pressure tactics, Harry,' I said. 'I understand in this business you're known as "The Closer".'

It went right past him. I sensed his enthusiasm had diminished somewhat, because as we approached the next prospective flat, Harry, who was driving me around in his gun-metal grey Talbot, actually said, 'I'll just wait in the car while you have a look.' He gave me the keys and I let myself in. The owner wasn't there, which was fine with me, because I didn't really want to meet (judging from the décor) a colour-blind Sherpa. The place was so depressing, so brown, so shitty – it reminded me of the house I had in the States. I walked out and resolved to redecorate when I got home.

On the way to the next place, I decided maybe what Harry needed was incentive. 'If it's any help, I'm prepared to pay cash,' I said.

This only made Harry more downcast. 'So you'll be looking for something to move into right away. Well I can't help you. Sorry. I'll just let you out near this mini-cab office.'

He slowed down to twenty, reached across my seat, opened the door and shoved me out.

Trudging back to my temporary rented waterbug palace, picking gravel from my teeth, I thought, am I the only one who finds it alarming that Brits entrust one of the biggest decisions of their lives to a stranger? (And by 'stranger' I mean a desultory, languorous dipweed who long ago gave up any spark of life in exchange for a lousy commission and an aquarium-eyed view of high-street punters.) Really, what are the qualifications for such a lofty position as Estate Agent?

1. Precise grasp of rudimentary muttering.
2. Natty ability to dress day after day in suits made of vague petroleum derivatives.
3. Know, *really know*, one's way around a photocopier

I've given up. I'm staying where I am. And please, if you're an estate agent reading this (yeah right), don't think you've stumbled on to a real lead and try to contact me, you oily barnacle. I've learned to accept my present hovel. Besides, as Elvis Costello says, 'Home is anywhere you hang your head.' Of course, he owns his home. Which is why he can say that.

ploughing suburbia

I'M CHUCK RUNION. What do you need to know about me? There's nothing much to say. I've lived here all my life. Graduated high school right up the road from where I live now. Four-bedroom ranchette with cedar-shake siding. Got a wife who drinks too much, kids who consider me an embarrassment, the whole shebang. Also, I'm kind of sensitive about my gums. By that, I don't mean I have sensitive gums. I mean I think my gums are a little too horsy. No one's ever said anything about it to my face, but it's not the kind of thing you would. Until last week.

Last Friday, two days before my fortieth birthday, Ned Lepper, my supervisor called me into his office. I work for DuPars Foods. Big kids' breakfast cereal outfit: Oat Rings, Wheat Rings, Choco Rings . . . we got 6% of the kiddie market. If you're wondering what the Kids' Cereal racket is like, one word: intense. Me, I'm just in product development – not a Player by any stretch of the imagination – but I'm close enough to the heat to know it can take a good man down before his time. Crunch and Crumble, we call it.

Anyhoo, Ned calls me in and sits me down. Ned's 'good people' – but a bit of a blowhard. He's got this annoying conversational habit of always saying 'anyway, to cut a long story short . . .' then leaving out *way* too much information. For instance, once we were down at Sovine's Tavern knocking back a few frosty ones and he comes out with:

'Chuck. Ever tell you about the time I went sport fishing in Bermuda? I had this charter boat and we're about fifteen miles out into the Atlantic when allofasudden this squall comes up and the captain says we gotta go back to the Marina. Well right then, wouldn't you know it, a two-hundred-pound tarpon hits my line, but the captain starts yelling at me, "Cut the line, cut it, for chrissakes, there's a squall comin' right for us!" And I says to him, "Look, Popeye, I'll be goddamned if I paid five-hundred dollars to come out to the middle of the Atlantic just to let a tarpon get away." So at this point the captain grabs a speargun and he aims it at *me* . . . anyway to cut a long story short, we end up living together on a houseboat in Amsterdam.'

'Whoa there, Ned,' I replied. 'I think you cut that story a little *too* short.'

But that's Ned Lepper for you. Anyway, I'm sitting there on his office couch and he looks me in the eye and says:

'You're a hell of an asset here, Chuck. The Niacin Enrichment thing you came up with last April . . . genius . . . can't believe I didn't think of that myself. Anyway . . . to cut a long story short . . . what's this about a Kiddie Porn Ring?'

'Beg your pardon?' I said.

Ned waved a piece of paper at me. 'This memo from your department proposing Kiddie Porn Rings . . .'

It took me a moment to figure it out. 'That's supposed to read Kiddie *Corn* Rings, Ned. It's a proposal for a new product.'

'Hmmm, *that's* a doozy of a misprint,' he said, slightly relieved. 'Well anyway, this morning your proposal came up at the stockholders meeting and 94% of them were dead set against Kiddie Porn.'

He stood up and, grimacing, walked over to me.

'In fact, they're out for your scalp, Chuck. I gotta let you go.'

'I'm *fired*?' I said, incredulously. This wasn't going well at all.

'Come on, Chuckee . . .' he said draping an arm over me. 'Don't beg. I'd let you come over and wax my car on weekends but that would be beneath you. Right?'

I cleaned out my desk and slouched outside to my car. My designated personal parking spot had already been re-assigned. Also, the carpark was being freshly repaved and no one had bothered to tell me. My car sat out there like a boat in a sea of wet cement. Once that stuff dried it was going to stick to my tyres and harden like a Flintstone car.

I called my wife, Louise, on the mobile and told her to come pick me up in the Tercel. I didn't tell her I'd just Crunched and Crumbled.

Lately, Louise had been acting a little flitty. When she picked me up, I detected a briny alcoholic tinge to her breath.

'Where have you been?' I said.

'Extension Class, where I go every Friday.'

'You smell like liquor.'

'Gloria Shipley and I made some moonshine.'

'*What?*' I said.

'Moonshine. White lightnin'. Pot liquor.'

'I thought you were taking the firewalking course.'

'There was a waiting list. So we signed up for home brewing. You been fired?' she asked, noticing my lifetime of work now sitting in a box on the back seat. Twelve years of brain racking, figuring out ways to vitamin-fortify pure sugar.

I told her what had happened. At first, she didn't believe it. Then, when I'd finally convinced her it was true, her expression turned to silent panic, a reaction I'd not expected. She used to tell me I should quit that job anyway. But now, looking at her eyes, I think she was watching the Gravy Train pull out of the station.

Her driving was fidgety. She kept checking her watch.

I punched up an oldies station on the radio. Louise punched it back to talk radio – *The Hello Henry Show*, some local gashead. I turned it down. The car was making clucking noises.

'When was the last time you changed the oil in this thing?' I asked. The Tercel was pretty dependable and I wanted to keep it that way. My car – the one in the wet cement – was a piece of shit. They could have it for all I cared.

'I like the oil that's in here,' she announced. Jesus, she was testy. Or tanked.

We inched along in the comatose traffic. Louise was trying to ease into the right lane, which would turn on to Darby Road, which would carry us home to Pepperidge Acres. Looking around I noticed practically every car had a *Baby On Board* sticker in the window.

'What do these people think *I'm* thinking?' I wondered aloud. 'That we'd *like* to plough into them but . . . oh look . . . they've got a baby on board. Well . . . in that case, never mind.'

I was trying to make a joke, to lighten up the atmosphere, but Louise seemed preoccupied.

Christ, the traffic was numbing. I tapped Louise on the shoulder and pointed to the Amoco Station on the corner.

'You could cut through the Amoco Station and save fifteen minutes!' I yelled.

With unexpected abandon, Louise lurched the car on to the Amoco lot and shot across, almost taking out the Blue Coral Washee-Waxee structure. Just as she was about to turn out on to Darby Road she slammed on the brakes. There was a highway patrol car right in front of us, stopped. The patrolman was eyeing us like a crocodile contemplating its prey. Neither of us was sure if cutting through an Amoco Station to avoid a red light was illegal or not, but I didn't need a confrontation, especially with Louise all tanked up on White Lightnin'. So she reversed around to the rear of the station and we sat there.

'Now what?' she said.

'Let me drive,' I said.

We switched places. The Amoco forecourt fed on to a Speedy Gonzales Auto Supply lot. Nothing separated them, so I eased on to the Speedy Gonzales lot and crept around behind the building, but when I came out on the other side, I could see the highway patrolman out on the main road, still keeping pace, watching us. The Speedy Gonzales lot fed into the Chipmunk Charlie's Pizza Emporium lot which fed into the Foofy-Burger lot which fed into the Wylie's World of Waterbeds lot which fed into the Mess O' Beefsteaks lot which fed into the Baken 'Em

Palace Olde Tyme English Muffin lot which fed into the Turtle World lot. So I wended around the parking islands and barriers and parked cars from one lot to another and the whole time the cop kept trolling along Darby Road, waiting for me to come out on to the highway.

'You know,' I said, 'I bet we could make it home if we just followed all these parking lots.'

'I'm sure we could,' said Louise 'But I'm not in the mood to play Magellan.'

'Seriously, this hooks up with the Partridge Acres Mall, and then there's that Japanese Steak House. If we get around that we hit the hospital. That's clear sailing . . .'

'Chuck, get serious. I've got things to do.'

'I *am* serious, Louise. It's a sea of concrete. Think of it. You and I, twenty-first-century explorers . . .'

'Chuck, get back on the highway.'

'. . . charting our own course.' I was easily doing thirty-five across the Mess O' Beefsteaks lot when I hit a speed bump, which jostled Louise violently. That's when she bolted from the car and lost herself amidst the crowd swarming to the Mess O' Beefsteaks Friday Night T-BoneAnza, leaving me alone in the Tercel.

I sat there, staring out at the glary, endless, relentless onslaught of stores, fast-food franchises, car dealerships, back pain clinics, the million useless, pointless, super-fluous amusements all sitting out there like a Retail Regatta on a Sea of Concrete. And it occurred to me that here, all around me, lay the swag, the breadwinnings, the *sustenance* that men, *responsible* men, were expected, as providers, to bring home. All this useless shit. And Louise, sensing it might no longer be forthcoming from me, had just bolted.

I set out, solo, on my forlorn challenge.

* * *

Look at all these saps in traffic going nowhere, I thought to myself. Ah, the joy of constant movement! The sun was declining now, mirrored in the chrome of parked cars. I marvelled at my own craftiness, stealing small advantages, navigating the lifeless maze of mobile homes at Two Ton Marty's Modular Lifestyles, carving my trail. The cop was still shadowing me. But because he was a highway patrolman, I'd deduced, he couldn't come on to private property. It was beyond his jurisdiction. So he was just waiting and licking his chops.

I ducked into the flow of drive-thru traffic at a Foofy-Burger.

'Can I have your order?' said a disembodied voice.

'Nothing thanks,' I replied into the speaker. 'Just passing through!'

At Fat Frankie's Trattoria, I surrendered the car to the mandatory valet parker, who transported it to the edge of the parking lot where I retrieved it. I didn't bother tipping him. Explorers don't tip. Magellan didn't tip. Behind the malls and discount houses and warehouses I passed the denizens of the town's commercial underbelly: boxcrushers, dumpstermen, treasure hunters, scroungers. I tooted the horn at every one of them and waved. When I reached a cross street, Euclid Avenue, I had to stop. It was public roadway. The cop was there, standing against his car, smirking.

'I see what you're trying to do, Runion,' he called out. 'You think you're sly. Come on this road and see how smart you really are.' He bared his crocodile grin. 'Sooner or later, Mr Big Gums, I'm gonna nail you.'

Unwritten rules had been established. I looked around and saw a soldier standing at a bus stop. I called over to him, asked him if he wanted a lift.

'You drive,' I yelled crisply and threw him the keys.

Instinctively, he took over the wheel. Good thing about soldiers, they're used to being barked at. You can use it to your advantage sometimes.

'Home on leave?' I asked as he pulled out on to Euclid Avenue.

'Yessir.'

'I was in the army myself. Fort Benning, Georgia. Hey, do my gums look big to you?'

'Sir?'

'Never mind.'

He guided the car across Euclid Avenue on to the lot of Wheeler Coberly's Chevrolet.

'Well, this is as far as I'm going,' I announced. 'Good luck, soldier!'

The soldier got out and headed back across the street to the bus stop.

At Wheeler Coberly's Chevrolet, a fleet of new cars blocked my path. Just like that bastard, Wheeler, to be overstocked, I thought. He always was Mr Slick. Even back in high school when he ran the yearbook and over-sold advertising space and every student's picture looked like an ad in the Yellow Pages.

The lights were still on in the showroom. Through the glass, I made out Wheeler beside a woman, his hands on her shoulders. Suddenly, he looked up and saw me out on the lot. Startled, both of them erupted into an almost comically choreographed attempt at hiding. The woman scuttled behind a new Impala and crouched. It was Louise.

Eventually Wheeler strolled out to the lot. He looked a little rattled.

'Hiya, Chuck!' he croaked. 'What brings you around?'

He still wore his big custom-made high school ring on his knuckle, an obscene cluster of metal with the school's insignia surrounding a fake opal. As far back as I can remember, he had an annoying habit of drilling it into a guy's shoulder as a way of greeting, which is what he did to me right then, although the gesture seemed flimsy. He knew I'd seen him with Louise.

I said, 'Listen, I got my eye on one of those spiffy new Blazers outside. Whaddya say to a test drive?'

Wheeler shifted uncomfortably in his loafers and looked at his watch.

'Christ, Chuck, it's pretty late,' he said.

'So? We'll open the moonroof.'

He shrugged and led me over to the row of Blazers and we climbed inside the nearest one. I started it up, pulled away, then abruptly stopped.

'Lemme just move my car, that all right with you?'

'Uh, sure,' said Wheeler. He was clearly puzzled. I got out, walked back towards my car, and caught a glimpse of my wife running out the showroom door into the night. Man, things sure can snowball, I thought to myself.

I edged the Tercel into the space left by Wheeler's Blazer and then we went for a test drive. We did that nine times in a row. Eventually I was able to move my car across the entire lot. Returning from test drive #9, Wheeler's patience had worn thin.

'You didn't really come here to buy a Blazer at all, did you, Chuck?'

I pushed the button on Wheeler's power seat console, causing his knees to crush against the dashboard. He winced.

'You screwing Louise, Wheeler?' I asked him.

Wheeler recoiled.

'I wouldn't screw *Louise*,' he said, as if the idea actually abhorred him. Somehow that made me even angrier.

55

Wheeler thumped my chest.

'I'm gonna take care of her. Look, you're not even supposed to know about this.'

So that was it. She'd already run to the comfort of someone else's arms.

'Well, when was I supposed to find out?'

'I dunno, Sunday? Listen, big fella . . .' Wheeler made an effort to sound consoling '. . . I heard the bad news about your job. That's why Louise is panicking right now. I told her "you gotta feel good about yourself." Even when times are bad, we gotta do *something* to feel good about ourselves, right, Chuck? So here's what I'm offering . . . 'cause I consider you a friend . . . You don't have to do a thing for a year. Understand? A whole year. That gives you time to get back on your feet.'

It was the craziest thing I'd ever heard.

Apparently, Wheeler Coberly was offering to take my wife off my hands for a year. I thought about it. *Really* thought about it. As long as he didn't try to bang her, what harm could it do? A year off from marriage could be a breath of fresh air.

'Whaddya say, Chuck? Can I tell her you said go for it?'

After a long thoughtful silence, I said, 'Promise you're not gonna try and screw her?'

Wheeler gestured toward the massive neon sign above the entrance. 'What does that say, Chuck? "Twenty-two Years of Integrity . . ."'

Delicately extracting himself from the car's deathgrip, Wheeler leaned his head back in through the window and winked.

'. . . *and* in the same location,' he said, and strode off.

I watched him head back to his gleaming, overlit

showroom. Louise was out there somewhere amongst the new cars, hiding. I pictured Wheeler, in his loafers, trying to calm her down, comfort her, slicktalk his way into her bellicose graces. I felt deflated. Like a bone-less chicken.

Out on the main drag, the cop car just sat there in black and white silence.

I focused on my expedition. I found ways through or around, forging ahead, ploughing through suburbia's fat harvest. The obstacles became more menacing. Construction sites, gravel pits, the Municipal Golf Course. At every side street I managed to solicit someone to drive me across.

'We heard about you on the radio,' said one volunteer ferryman. 'Good Luck!'

That explained the helicopter that had materialised above me while I was circumnavigating the sandtrap at the 14th hole. The Radio 90 Newsbird! I'd thought it was the police. I turned on the car radio and there was Hello Henry, that bloated gashead, calling me 'an urban trailblazer, a local folk hero . . .' Indeed, there was a smattering of onlookers starting to line my path now, cheering me on. Out on the road a string of cop cars now ran alongside. Apprised of my ridiculous escapade, they'd come to see for themselves, Chuck Runion – Twenty-first Century Explorer.

But when the commercial sprawl gave way to the rectangular tyranny of split-level ranchettes, and I began to trundle across people's front lawns like a Panzer Tank, I was no longer folk hero. I became a public menace. Homeowners emerged from their houses and cursed me. It just egged me on. I felt the satisfying crunch of someone's skateboard beneath my tyres. Too bad, kid, I thought to myself, you'll just have to pick up your life and start all over again. I churned across driveways and hedges, gladiolas and garden gnomes, while their owners, scattering like tenpins, wondered what kind of nutcake would scar their little quarter-acre dream.

Then, my own cedar-shaked house came into view. Out in the driveway, crowned with a big red birthday bow, sat a Wheeler Coberly Chevrolet, showroom fresh. There beside it stood Wheeler himself. And Louise and the kids. I realised then what was going on. Louise had bought me a new car for my birthday, but after she found out I'd been shitcanned, she'd panicked and run back to Wheeler's to cancel the sale. And then I'd shown up, purely by accident. *That whole conversation with Wheeler was about buying a car.*

They watched, pityingly, my approach. Whatever conspired elation of gift-giving they may have hoped to share was now squandered by my erratic arrival. They were just shaking their heads.

I looked over at the house, tried to remember what it felt like when we first moved in. But it just seemed like it had always been there, with its smell of sour kidfunk and cooking sherry: the three-piece Ethan Allan nautical-themed, maple living-room suite and the framed K-Mart portrait on the mantle: Louise and me, embracing in front of some fake studio clouds. I thought about how no one, until today, had ever mentioned aloud how big my gums were. I stared into the rearview mirror and, yeah, I had to admit, they looked like canned Spam. So right before I reached my own front lawn I just pulled that Tercel out on to the street and kept going until Louise and Wheeler disappeared in my rearview mirror. You two can have each other, I said to myself. Besides, she didn't have that new-wife smell anymore.

Anyway, to cut a long story short . . . I'm living on a houseboat in Amsterdam.

great jokes squandered

Disaster in Dublin

P OTENTIALLY, IT WAS one of the Greatest Jokes of All Time.

An old fella ambles into a bar. He's carrying a paper bag. 'Man o' man, could I use a drink,' he says to the bartender. 'Ain't got no money but I can show you a great trick.'

It's a slow afternoon so the bartender says, 'Okay, if it's a great trick,' and pours him a drink.

The old guy takes his time, relishing every drop. Finally, when he's done, he walks over to an old upright piano in the corner, reaches into his bag and pulls out a large green bullfrog. He sits it on the edge of the piano and commands, 'Play!'

The frog launches into a spirited, note-perfect ragtime number.

'Unbelievable!' yells the astonished bartender and pours

61

the man a second drink, on the house. 'How'd he do that?'

'Trained him myself,' said the old guy. 'Now, for a sandwich, I'll show you another trick.'

The bartender disappears, then returns with a sandwich. He waits for the old guy to finish it. Then the old guy goes back over to the piano, reaches into his bag again and pulls out a big rat, which he sits on top of the piano.

'Sing!' he yells, and unbelievably, whilst the frog plays, the rat belts out a lusty version of 'Mood Indigo'. The bartender is floored.

'Unbelievable,' he says again.

Suddenly, mid-song, the barroom door swings open and in walks a Hollywood agent. He is astounded by what he sees. He's never seen a singing rat or a piano-playing frog before. He rushes over to the old man.

'You own these creatures?' he asks.

'Sure do,' answers the old guy.

'I'll give you $500,000 for the pair,' he says.

The old guy shakes his head.

'I'm fairly partial to 'em,' he says.

'$750,000!' says the agent.

'I don't know . . .'

'Listen . . .' says the agent. 'I won't take "no" for an answer. How much just for the rat?' He's thinking he could get someone to accompany the rat on piano.

The old guy thinks about it. Finally, 'Well I suppose I could let it go for a million.'

'Deal!' says the agent and writes him a cheque on the spot.

The bartender watches the agent leave carrying the rat with him.

'Why didn't you sell the frog?' he asks. 'You could've got another million dollars, at least.'

'Oh, I'd never sell this frog,' he says. 'He's too good a ventriloquist.'

Like I said, potentially one of the Greatest Jokes of All Time. Unfortunately, it never happened. A great joke is a beautiful thing. When it works – when the characters are compelling, the setting well established, the implausibility and timing melding together in perfect conjunction – well it's a small miracle. But, sadly, a lot of great jokes get flubbed in the execution.

The 'Frog/Rat' Joke was supposed to take place at three p.m. on 17 May 1995 in a reliable bar called Feeny's in Dublin, Ireland. I know, because I was there at the end of the bar, minding my own business, when it all went down. Feeny's has been the setting for some very successful jokes, notably the immortal 'Frank, I think we found the fella who pissed in your tuba!' (11 March 1991.)

The bartender in the joke, Eammon Langton, was also a reliable pro. You may remember him as the guy who wisecracked, 'We don't get many crocodiles ordering screwdrivers in this bar' in 'At these prices, I can under-stand why!' (14 June 1989.) Given the solid characteri-sation and believable setting, everything should have gone to snuff. The problem was with the frog.

Essentially, he blew it from the beginning. He breezed into the bar at two forty-five p.m., hopped up on to the barstool and said, 'Hey, where the hell *is* everyone?', thus effectively killing the surprise element of a Talking Bullfrog.

'Whaddya know?' said Eammon. 'A talking frog.'

'Yeah, they sent me over to be in a joke,' said the frog. 'Guess I'm a little early. Fix me up with a pint, will ya?'

The frog was semi-legless when the old man burst through the door carrying the paper bag.

'What the fuck are you doing!' he yelled at the frog. 'You're supposed to be in this bag.' Then he turned to the bartender. 'Did he *talk* to you already? Oh, for the love of Christ!'

'Watch your mouth, fella,' slurred the frog. 'I won't be in a joke if there's profanity.'

The bartender, ever the consummate professional, sticks to his lines. 'Okay. If it's a great trick,' he says, and pours the old man a drink.

The old man finishes the drink then grabs the frog by his throat and walks over to the corner of the bar.

'MMMMMMMMPH,' gasps the gurgling frog, Guinness dribbling from its mouth.

The old man stops and looks around. 'Where the hell's the piano!' he shrieks. 'There's *supposed* to be a piano!'

'We sent it out to be restrung,' replies the bartender. 'You owe me a punt for the beer.'

It got worse. The Hollywood agent called to say he had ended up in the wrong joke. His car had broken down near a farmhouse and he had been forced to spend the night in a barn with a pig and a sheep. He apologised for not making the joke, but it didn't matter anyway. It had all fallen apart.

Me, I finished my drink and quietly left. Sometimes you get the joke, sometimes you don't.

If Police Wrote Jokes

Official Constabulary Report of joke purported to take place in Serenghetti precinct, 17 October 2002

Case 17659: Gorilla/Lion Incident
On or about 1100 hrs. morning of 17 Oct. complainant, hereto referred to as 'Gorilla' (no fixed address, 6 ft 8 in.

hght., app. wght. 380 lbs, eyes: black, wearing dark fur coat), was engaged in pursuit of 'Rabbit', hereto referred to as Witness (no fixed address, 7 in. hght., app. wght. 4.5 lbs, eyes: pink, wearing white fur coat), for said purpose of consumption, in vicinity of Plot 117-a, Quadrant 4, NW Vector, near big pile of rhinoceros shit.

Gorilla was approaching Rabbit when Rabbit entered hole. Gorilla attempted to follow suit. Hole was apparently too restrictive to accommodate Gorilla, whose head became intractably lodged. Removal could not be negotiated.

Said Gorilla claims to have been trapped in hole, in less than dignified position, for almost two hours. At no time was Gorilla offered aid, comfort or rescue by any passersby.

On or about 1300 hrs. Lion, hereto referred to as Suspect (no fixed address, Occupation: 'King' (????), 5ft 1 in. hght., app. wght. 550 lbs, blond features), happened upon scene and without provocation or premeditation did engage in beastly sexual act with Gorilla and without Gorilla's consent (Violation 317 – Forcible and Cowardly Lion Conduct).

Said Lion did continue wanton and immoral act for roughly twenty minutes while Gorilla struggled to defend itself while head was still stuck in hole.

Lion then, whether sated or distracted, disengaged itself from Gorilla and fled scene of crime. It was at this point that a humiliated, justifiably enraged Gorilla was able to extricate itself from hole and pursue Lion.

Ensuing chase covered extensive length of Savannah and was witnessed by several giraffes, a python and at least twelve meerkats (see attached depositions), whose accounts corroborate complainant's story.

Near Plot 216-B, by gooma-gooma trees, Lion

managed to elude Gorilla and disappear from sight.

At this point Lion, likely fearing retribution, did enter a canvas tent belonging to one Dr Niles Brubaker, an epidemiologist from Columbia University, NY (Note: such entry constitutes violation of Jungle Code 117-F: Forcible Entry.) Dr Brubaker was not present at time of entry and, as such, Lion ransacked premises, appropriating a pith helmet and a newspaper and did occupy Dr Brubaker's canvas-backed chair. Donning the pith helmet and pretending to read the newspaper, Lion waited, anticipating Gorilla's arrival. (Violation of Jungle Code 156: Impersonating a Medical Officer Under False Pretenses.) Said Lion was engaged in aforementioned fraudulent behaviour when Gorilla entered tent, looked around and said, 'Sir, have you seen a Lion run by?' to which Lion replied, 'You mean the one that buggered you?' to which Gorilla replied, 'My God, it's already made the papers?'

Previous complaints and convictions: Abovementioned Lion has been reported engaging in illegal sexual conduct on several occasions, most notably 12 July 2001 (near Plot 342-A) where Lion was observed having sexual relations in the open with a Giraffe, although said relations appeared to be consensual. It was during this act that Lion was heard to remark to Giraffe, 'Uh oh, here comes my wife. Make it look like I'm eating you.'

evolution in reverse

THE STATE SENATE of Kansas has put forward a bill making it a crime to teach Evolution in public schools. Go back and reread this sentence, just to make sure it says what you thought it says. Obviously, anyone who would pass that kind of law is in an advanced state of evolutional decline. And in order to de-evolve, one must have *evolved* (to a certain level), which, at least, *proves* Evolution. So there.

Anyway, Kansans – when they're not travelling on broomsticks in tornados – like to think of themselves as staunch family types with Spartan, stalwart religious values. They don't want their kids studying cavemen or monkeys. One plink of the senate gavel will effectively eliminate the need to teach Anthropology, Early Civilisation, Middle-Eastern History, Comparative Religious Studies and, of couse, Zoology and Evolutionary Science. And that's saving a lot of money!! Also it leaves more time for practical instruction in Auto Repair or Football Tackling.

You would think kids today are savvy enough to form their own beliefs as to whether man arrived through a protracted process of natural selection or simply materialised from a lightning bolt off the tip of God's finger. But the Kansas department of public schools would prefer its students not haggle with such trivialities. It hasn't occurred to them that most kids today are far more familiar with a Playstation manual than the Scripture. Any eight-year-old can create a Knockout Kings boxer in his own image or the image of anyone else. But getting his boxer to the top requires a deft talent for strength, self-preservation and survival, an argument for evolution far more entertaining than protracted viewings of *Inherit the Wind*.

Why aren't Kansas students allowed to formulate their own opinions about where they came from? How do these self-righteous, bible-thumping, baby-dunking, big-haired, sharp-shooting Senators for God get elected into decision-making positions?

Kansas, for all its uninterrupted landscape, is an astoundingly narrow-minded place. It's all corn and silage, dragstrips and Baptist churches. It has produced such dynamically opposed bastions of blandness as Ike Eisenhower (America's most boring President) to Kansas (America's most boring prog rock band) to Pizza Hut (America's most boring chain of pizzas). Tornados generally do little damage to Kansas as they tend to die quickly of boredom and inertia. Perhaps the Kansas Senate has nothing better to do than sit around contemplating the existence of men, and because monkeys aren't indigenous to the area, it doesn't have to get too distracted from its tenacious biblical roots. But give me an affable chimp in a bellman's outfit any day over the granite-beaked, beady-eyed fundamentalist of America's Midwest. Chimps don't bomb abortion clinics. God must look down on all the televangelized legions of Right Wingers in America and think, 'Man, o' man, I can't believe these clowns are playing for my team.'

Maybe it's better to view Human Evolution on a peaked graph, as opposed to an upwardly linear one. We have, in two thousand years, perfected a technology of unimaginable potential, yet mostly we just use it to make animals move their lips in TV adverts. My own view of human development is best demonstrated as follows:

Find one of those 'Ages of Man' charts – the one that progresses from a gangly chimp to a fully developed Homo Sapien. Draw a little television remote control in the hand of each figure. Then hold the chart up to a mirror. Surprise! You're in Kansas.

go home and practise

PRACTICALLY EVERY KID in America who ever owned a guitar learned to play using the Chick Spofford Ezee Manual 'Guitar Playing for Beginners'. As an instructor, he has coached countless budding young musicians through their first faltering chords. This, arguably, makes Chick Spofford the most imitated, if not the most famous, guitarist in the world. Here, he indulges in a wistful reverie of his substantial achievements.

I was sitting at home one Saturday watching Lawrence Welk when I got a trunk call from England. That's what we called them back then – trunk calls. This would have been '68, hell, maybe '69. Not important. Anyhoo, this voice comes over the line:

'Chick, this is Hendrix. You gotta help me, man.'

'Who?' I says.

'Hendrix . . . c'mon, dude . . . it's Jimi. Listen, I've forgotten "A".'

I remembered him. Seattle kid. Had an enormous thumb and he was, I tell you, bone idle lazy. Never really got with the program as far as students go. I could hear people chanting his name in the background and he sounded a bit distraught.

'I'm at the Isle of Wight . . .' he said, which meant zippedydoodah donuts to me, I never heard of the damn place.

'I'm 'bout to go onstage and for the life of me, "A" has slipped my fuckin' mind. You gotta help me!'

'Jimi,' I says, 'have you been practising your triads like I told you to?'

'Man, that was seventeen years ago!' he screamed back. Always was wrapped a little to tight, you ask me. 'Chrissakes, Chick, can ya' just talk me through the "A" chord?'

I'm not usually lenient. What I shoulda done was make him do his scales right there over the phone, do-re-mi up and down the frets for an hour. But it was an expensive call and I could hear all them folks yellin' for him . . . so I figured what the hey, and just told him where to put his fingers and he thanked me and hung up and a year or so later the fella was dead. Drugs, I heard. Wouldn't of happened if he'd stayed in his room and practised . . .

I don't care if you're Eric Clapton or Andre Segovia or Joey Kissmyyankeewhiteass – you do your triads and you do your first positions, then you go back, Jack, and do it again and *you make sure they're clean*. It's like this Neil Young fella on the radio. How many years has he been playin' guitar . . . thirty?! Christ almighty I never heard such a godawful racket in my life! All that buzzing and distortion and humbucking and the kids all whooping and cheering like he's pulling goddamn lightning out of his ass or something and all I can think is 'That idiot isn't pressing his damn strings down all the way, the lazy bastard.' 'Rust never sleeps' my ass. Sounds to me like Rust never practises. I used to give my students a tennis ball to walk around with and squeeze so they'd develop some wrist muscle. You don't develop your wrists, you gonna get that buzzin' sound on the neck every time. Lazy, limp-wristed pansies. Go home and practise! 'Scuse me for sayin' so.

I been teaching the Chick Spofford Ezee Method for sixty-three years, come this October. Served as a signal corpman in World War II in Germany, during the Occupation. We used to sit around them bierhauses listening to that infernal oom-pah rubbish all the time and I'd get sick of it and go looking for a guitar to strum. But there weren't many around in those days on account of most guitars was Spanish and Spain was neutral during the war or somethin' like that . . . anyhoo, I'd end up having to jerryrig a guitar out of an empty cigar box and a flyswatter, strung with whatever whiskers I could nick off an itinerant alleycat, plus some tuning pegs you could usually find in someone's old knickknack drawer, and of course somebody would always have a spare saddle and bridge lying around and a rudimentary carving form for shaping the sound-hole, then I would put a nice rose-wood veneer on to it – you know, nothing too fancy – then we would buff it out, fret it, tune it to 440 hertz which was the standard pitch back during the Big Two and I'd sit on the barstool and play 'Jenny Lind' and that, mister, is what passed for entertainment in those days.

*   *   *

People ask me why I don't tour more often. It ain't because I do so well with the manuals and teaching lessons, which I do, thankyouverymuch for asking. You wanna know the truth, I ain't that great a live performer. I'm a chord man, pure and simple. You want a Bminor7, I'll give you a note-perfect Bminor7. But I was never all that good at stringing together all those chords into what they call 'songs'. Some outfit called Porno for Pyros asked me to tour with them a few years back, as an opening act. The lead singer – never did get his name – claimed I was one of his big influences. I figured what the hell, I'd give it a whirl. Well don't you know I found myself standing in front of 5,000 screaming hopheaded jackasses and showed every one of 'em how to play a perfect diminished C7. I think I lasted all of thirty seconds. They practically ripped me to pieces, ungrateful bastards. Hell, half of 'em probably owned my book at one time or another. 'Go home and practise, you lazy twits!!' is what I yelled at 'em. Least that's the last thing I remember, anyhow.

Now if you'll excuse me, I gotta go practise my triads. 'Physician heal thyself.' Know what I'm saying?

but the Bible is actually rife with sarcasm, '*Mary rode Joseph's ass all the way to Bethlehem*' (Luke 34:23) being a good example. (She was pregnant and they had no inn reservations on a holiday weekend. Obviously the woman was in a foul mood.)

The reference to Jesus as a carpenter may have been a weak attempt at irony. In Isaiah (44:9:20) one can read:

All who make idols are nothing . . . the carpenter measures with a line, makes an outline with a compass. He shapes it in the form of a man and worships it. He knows nothing, understands nothing. His eyes are plastered over so he cannot see. Don't quote me on that.

When Jesus, as a young phenom, returned to his home town of Nazareth, he didn't exactly receive a rousing welcome. Townspeople wanted to see him perform some of his lauded feats, but he just took it easy. *"'I've seen better Miracles with Smokey Robinson", spoke Luther'* (Mark 5:7). Again, pure sarcasm. So Jesus was seen as nothing special by the people, and calling him a 'carpenter' was akin to calling him a nobody. Jesus, unflappable, just took it in his stride and continued his itinerant preaching.

What the man did have was good contacts. His father Joseph was a very respected craftsman. People expected the same quality work from his kid. Immaculate conception, it stood to reason, should have resulted in immaculate construction, but sadly that wasn't the case, which is why no legacy of Jesus' carpenterial efforts exists today.

The truth is, given his busy miracle-working and other good works, Jesus wasn't 'on-site' that often. Like most well-known builders, he left most of the work to subcontractors. In other words, Jesus didn't really build things any more than Eddie Stobart actually drives trucks. These subcontractors, knowing clients had paid good money expecting Christ to perform the work on their house, often tried to pass themselves off as 'Jesus'. They wore beards and sandals and spoke in vague parables (a good way of keeping clients confused about expenses). Thus, in building circles, they were referred to as 'B-Jesuses' – substandard Jesuses. Their work, which was usually haphazard and shoddy, often led to fisticuffs with irate homeowners, hence the term 'to whomp the Bejesus out of someone'.

Now, here's where science and religion shake hands and sit down to a cup of hot coffee. Though the B-Jesuses have long since disappeared, the word B-Jesus (or Bejesus) still exists today not just as a colloquialism, but as an actual physical entity. Bejesus exists in microscopic amounts in all of us and kind of resembles chalk dust. It was first detected in the human body by an Irish physiologist, Dr Brian Cromarty, who was conducting experiments at Dublin's Trinity College in 1927. Dr Cromarty, a devout but practical man, theorised that since God gave Jesus to all of us as a gift, and since Jesus died, then returned, he probably divided himself up into practically everybody. Thus, factored into a human population of, say, 6 billion, the amount of Bejesus in any of us is about .000000006% . . . a fairly negligible trace, far less than, say, Niacin. But it can be extracted.

If you really want to see Bejesus, try punching someone really hard in the face. Bejesus will appear as a fine, almost microscopic white mist flying off their heads. This action usually results in the person punched actually announcing that he has had the 'Bejesus knocked out of him.' If this strikes you as harsh, you can also try

we're not the kennedys

'M NOT SO quick to buy into the premise of the
Kennedy's being America's 'Royal' Family. Take away
the racketeering, bootlegging, gerrymandering, bimbo-
wrangling, mafia liaisons and chronic alcoholism, and
they're really just the folks next door. Nor do I believe
they're 'cursed'. Stupidity isn't a curse. It's just stupidity.
Every family tree has a few branches that have un-
ceremoniously snapped off. You just don't hear about
them because they're not in the public eye.

You could deduce, in the grim genealogical tableau of
my own family, several Kennedyesque traits. One, we're
a predominately male-oriented family, meaning the
women have kept low public profiles and avoided the
derision that seems to follow the rest of us around. Also,
like the Kennedys, the tragedies in our family have mostly
targeted men. Like my cousin Dwight, who was 'cursed'
with the misfortune of once calling a barroom full of
Gypsy Joker bikers a 'simpering passel of Kansas City

Faggots', eloquently posited but wrong on a whole lot of different levels. It was a tragic end for a man who, in addition to his full-time pursuit of 'drifting', had recently shaken things up in the KKK organisation.

Frankly, I see the whole Kennedy 'curse' as something easily avoidable. It has to do with water. Since Edward Kennedy's Chappaquiddick incident in the sixties (he was carrying a mysterious female passenger in his car when he plunged into a river – she drowned), we've seen William Kennedy Smith accused of attempted rape on a beach in Florida, John Kennedy Jr plummeting his plane into the sea near Martha's Vineyard, and Michael Kennedy perishing in a ski (read frozen water) accident.

It seems obvious to me you have to keep the Kennedys away from H_2O. In other words, don't get 'em wet. (Remember that movie *Gremlins*?)

In my own family, water hasn't figured quite as prominently or tragically. Well, there *was* my Uncle Roman.

Uncle Roman sold swimming pools door-to-door. He used to take me cold-calling with him. I was eight or nine at the time. We would arise early, eat pancakes, then climb inside his panel van, which had 'Pirate Pete's Pools' stencilled on the side and featured a one-eyed, peg-legged parrot as a mascot. Why a half-blind, feathered amputee was chosen to represent a pool company was never explained.

Uncle Roman smelled like Aqua-Velva. He generally wore a loud – very loud – Hawaiian shirt. He was lanky and gregarious and, as far as I know, had never actually immersed himself in a swimming pool. Still, he claimed to be Pirate Pete's number one 'closer'. I believed him. We would trawl the new housing developments on the outskirts of town, the ones with idyllic names like 'Breton Forest' or 'Wandering Wisteria Menthol Canyon Estates' – names thought up, no doubt, by the wives of the developers. Uncle Roman would park the panel van at the top of the street and we would set out on foot, 'punching doorbells'.

'Aloha, Mahalo!' he would yell to bemused house-wives standing sentry-like in their doorways, usually with a grenade cluster of curlers in their hair. 'My name is Roman Figgatt and I need you to help send me to Hawaii!' It was a canny sales tactic designed to put the householder on the charitable offensive. Roman would then explain he was only one swimming pool sale away from a free trip to Honolulu, for himself and his family.

'Kid's never seen the ocean,' he would say, indicating me. My part was to look forlorn and land weary.

Eventually he would worm his way around to the backyard, where he would talk the housewife through a verbal excavation of the premises, and paint for her a vivid shimmery poolside scenario – sparkling, azure waters, the gleeful shrieks of frolicking sprogs, cabanas and cool lemonades, a respite from the thick, insuffer-able humidity of the oncoming summer. ('The hottest on record. That's what they're saying.') The capper, once the image was firmly planted in the housewife's head, was to winsomely explain The Pirate Pete's 6-Point Easy Payment Plan.

As an eight-year-old, I was baffled that anyone could say no to Uncle Roman's proposal. It seemed to me the dream of owning a swimming pool was the reason people got up to go to work in the morning and pursued their lives. I didn't know what I know now, which is that swimming pools are one of the quintessential obnoxities of the free world. They are fetid chemical containers,

81

dubiously constructed and generally ill-maintained. For some reason, they symbolise America's Leisure Class Dream. But basically, they're just Big Blue Urinals.

Later in the afternoon, Roman would follow up his 'bites', returning to talk to the Man of the House. He would cajole a cup of coffee, sit down and seriously explain how a swimming pool increased a property's value and gave it 'kerb appeal' (even though it was in the back yard). He never took rejection seriously.

As the summer languished, however, I began to notice that Uncle Roman's 'territory' seemed to be trajecting outwardly. By July we were driving well past the new subdivisions to semi-rural areas, where the houses were squat and non-descript and smelled cabbagey. More people here slammed doors in Roman's face.

By late August we were up into the mountain hamlets. Here the houses were spindly, some of them just tar-paper shacks. I was beginning to wonder if maybe Uncle Roman was a pretty crap salesman and these longer drives amounted to a demotion.

'The best salesman gets the toughest territory,' he would say. It never really occurred to me that he was *reliant* on selling pools – to put food on the table for his own family. I kinda thought he did it because, he was, well, divinely empowered to *offer* people swimming pools. In other words, he seemed to me to possess low-level super-power qualities. Of course I also believed that about the guy who drove the neighbourhood ice-cream truck. Until it turned out he was a child molester.

In these more 'rustic' areas, Uncle Roman had come up with a new sales tactic. He would pull out a large writing pad and rather floridly total up the costs of installing the pool, making a seemingly oblivious mathematical error the customer couldn't help but notice:

'Lessee, that's . . . $500 for excavation, $500 for installation. $250 for the Custom Concrete Non-Slip Patio Surfacing . . . $320 for labour and I throw in the filter pump. That comes out to . . . hmmmmm . . . carry the seven . . . $1,070.'

Quite often, the customer took 'advantage' of Uncle Roman's mistake.

One day we drove up to a place called Hazard and Uncle Roman pulled on to a long dirt road winding past dilapidated tractor parts and sad fence line. We pulled up to a hillside shack sitting on stilts, like a dry-docked boat. It was straight out of Dog Patch, USA. There was a kid on the porch in huge wadded nappies balancing, in his hands, a hamburger the size of his head. He eyed us defensively. Looking around us, I didn't see much poolside potential. Then a man in a cap advertising chewing tobacco appeared from around the side of the shack. Uncle Roman got out of the van and the two walked a distance away. There was a heated, animated exchange between them. Uncle Roman pulled out his pad and several minutes later I heard the man say, 'What kind of fool do you think I am?' to which Uncle Roman replied, perhaps a mite too affably, 'Well, what are the categories?' The man turned and hastened toward his porch and Uncle Roman scuttled just as quickly back to the van. The kid on the porch just stood there holding his gigantic hamburger, sizing up the situation and idly banging his face into the sandwich's contents.

Uncle Roman had just turned the ignition when a bullet exploded the rear windscreen. 'Uh oh,' he said, and drove like Jehu roaring down the track, dust billowing through the window like a broken vacuum cleaner. It wasn't till we were almost home that I noticed he'd wet his trousers. He noticed I'd noticed. 'Have the decency not to say anything to your folks,' he said. The following week he turned in the Pirate Pete van and took a job managing Manny's Blue Coral Three-Minute Car Wash. I guess it kept him near the water.

Then there was my uncle Jerome, who exemplified that life is nothing but eating, smoking, napping and Looking Forward to the Next Big Thing. A flintier man you've never met. Too cheap to marry, he lived most of his life in a one-bedroom shotgun apartment above a dentist's office, which he shared with my twin aunts Elsie and Lessie, spinster nurses. The apartment had a pervasive medicinal atmosphere. It smelled of cloves, Lysol disinfectant and singed tooth enamel. It was always spotless, because my twin aunts were sterile.

Uncle Jerome, poor sod, slept on a couch in the hallway next to the kitchen, with all his possessions kept in a suitcase beneath the couch. So I suppose you could say he pretty much *lived* on the couch. His path to either the kitchen or the toilet was covered in old newspapers that my aunts had laid down as if he were unhousebroken. He spent most of his time lying around reading Erskine Caldwell novels while Elsie and Lessie flitted about attempting to disinfect him. Every year as a Christmas gift he gave everyone Gideon bibles, which, I suspect, he had pilfered from hotel rooms. He was a postman. Not remotely religious.

The bitterest edict in his life was that my aunts absolutely forbade him to smoke cigarettes or drink Old Granddad inside the apartment (which, by the way, he *owned*). They would shoo him out on to the front porch, downstairs. Unfortunately the dentist – his tenant – didn't want some cigarette-smoking, Old-Granddad-reeking coot lurking around his porch. Bad for business. So *actually* what my uncle had to do was go out to the pavement to smoke/drink, but the pavement had been upended into chunky hillocks by the roots of the overgrown oak trees lining the street, so *really* what my Uncle Jerome had to do was cross the street and stand in front of the Brown Proctor Funeral Home just to enjoy a goddamned puff/snort. His one daily pleasure in life and he had to hike fifty yards to do it! No wonder he was cranky all the time.

But the most amazing thing about Uncle Jerome – whom I never saw squander so much as a dime, who was so tightfisted that if he removed a five-dollar bill from his wallet, Abe Lincoln would have squinted at the light – this same man, once a year, would take a holiday to Tahiti, or book himself on the *QEII* or go skiing in Gstaad! I swear to God. He would just cut loose. He would return two weeks later, tanned and hale, a regular Mr Continental. He always brought back photos of himself: Uncle Jerome gamboling in Caribbean waters, Uncle Jerome jockeying the baccarat tables at Monte Carlo. Once he showed me a photo of himself alongside David Niven, both in black tie attire. They looked like best friends. He kept the pictures in a cigar box underneath the couch he lived on for the other fifty weeks of the year. I suppose it was those two weeks of Corbel and coq-au-vin – the Next Thing To Look Forward To – that allowed him to put up with news-lined trails to the toilet the rest of the time.

Our primary family activity was going to the drive-in movies. Maybe this seems like fun to Brits because Britain doesn't have drive-ins and it all sounds like some wistful bit of Americana but, believe me, it was hell six ways from Sunday. When I'm in a car the prominent thought going through my head is jeez o' man, I wish I wasn't in a car, so the memory of being crammed into a vehicle with a herd of relatives for an entire double feature, is a fairly wretched one.

First of all, I grew up in the South – North Carolina and Tennessee – where it gets so hot you'd gladly wrap your lips around a trailer hitch if you thought it would drag you north to Canada. Pieces of your thigh stick to the vinyl of car seats, then peel like strip bacon. Sometimes people would turn to petroleum byproducts right in front of your eyes. And on nights like these, when as John Prine would say, 'the fans were in the window and the door propped open with a broom', my parents, granddad, various aunts and uncles would think it was the greatest idea in the world to fire up the Plymouth and trundle down to the drive-in, which charged a dollar a carload. Even Uncle Jerome would come along. Naturally, he reeked of Old Granddad. (Old Granddad, incidentally, is a bourbon, and not to be confused with my Old Granddad who reeked of Jim Beam, a different bourbon entirely.) You can imagine my hairy, bulbous-featured relatives, sweating like mastodons, squirming and ululating around me, while vinyl stripped my flesh, my mother cradling some steamy rancid butter-bag of homemade popcorn *because my family was too cheap to buy it from the snack bar*, and my Aunt Nelta, who had some medical condition that made her continuously burp egg yolk-like emanations in my general direction – this is what I was up against at the drive-in. A real Donkey Ride to Hell.

The drive-in, whose marquee display always looked like it was maintained by a ransom-note specialist, would be advertising odd combinations: *The Sound of Music* and *Gutbucket of Blood*, for example. Once ensconced on the gravel forecourt for the night, Mom would put me outside, on a blanket, in front of the car, so the rest of the family could have what she called 'grown-ups' time'.

'Grown-ups' time' usually consisted of the lot of them mixing up Jim Beam and Pepsi into an army surplus canteen and passing it around until everyone was good and soused, and then Uncle Jerome would start referring to all women within earshot as 'whores'. Then my grandfather, who owned a small nuclear plant and was always concerned about 'leaving the rods alone for too long', would start fretting about meltdown.

So, as if it weren't hot enough already, I had to sit there on a blanket on the gravel *in front of the Plymouth's grille*, which, fresh from its journey, was still spewing heat, right against my head. I wasn't allowed to leave because my mother was convinced I'd get lost or kidnapped. I couldn't even watch the film because of the rivulets of sweat cascading down into my eyes.

And that is the watery tragedy of my life.

About halfway into the first feature, everyone inside the Plymouth would be overcome by the need for a pee, so they would pile out of the car in a chunderous display of Neanderthal pageantry and clamber off to the toilets, except for my grandfather, who was too old to make the trip and at this point had consumed enough Jim Beam to no longer care about radioactivity.

Returning from the *en masse* piss expedition, Uncle Jerome could always be counted on to linger in front of the projection shack to make obscene shadow puppets, which set off a cacophony of car horns and, on more than one occasion, a fist fight.

Afterwards, when everyone was dehydrated and drunk beyond human limits, Uncle Jerome would take us to a

the meat hat marches on

A S FASHION ECHOES the trends of humankind, so has the meat hat mirrored the vagaries of butcherdom. If there is a snappier dressed professional than the British Meatcutter, I have yet to meet him. Decked out in his crisp white smock and sharp-peaked hat, the butcher *cuts* (sorry) a pretty sharp figure. Even if he is spackled in blood and gristle.

The meat hat itself is more or less a tidemark of the climactic changes meatcutting has undergone in its history, and – to me at least – it is fascinating to chart the subtle changes in its shape and appearance throughout the years.

1926: Emergence of the modern meat hat. In a year of economic strife and mass unionisation, the meat hat is adopted as a unified standard of dress for butchers throughout Britain. It signifies solidarity, but with a touch of panache.

1928: Astounding news!! The completion of the National Herd Book!! Virtually every cow in Britain is accounted for. The meat hat takes on a more festive appearance.

1929: Crash of Wall Street reverberates through Britain. Economic slump is reflected in the more austere design of the meat hat.

1939–1940: World War II breaks out. Channel Islands occupied by German forces. The vaguely Tyrollean shape of the meat hat does nothing to help its image. It now has traitorous implications.

1948: Electricity nationalised. Hooray!! Advent of the electric meat saw. Meatcutting moves into the future and so does the hat.

1956: Cornish Backlash. Ginsters of Cornwall strikes the first blow in mass-marketed Meat Revolution by inventing the take-home pie. The hat is now worn defensively, almost in a military fashion.

1964: Pig Breeding Stock on the decline. Lamb Cutlets subjected to withering criticism. Friction amongst Charolais and Friesians serves as an apt metaphor for the Cuban Missile Crisis and the Cold War. McDonald's opens in America. The meat industry is at its nadir. Meat hat valiantly resists the seemingly endless onslaught of bad news.

1971: First purebred Limousin bulls and heifers arrive at Leith Docks in Edinburgh. The hardiness, durability and easy calving qualities of this breed will result in a tender and glorious marbled steak. This is the golden age of Meat in Britain! The hat is now a celebratory plume of self-congratulation.

1996: Twenty-five years of prosperity come to an end. Major outbreak of Vesticular Stomatitis. Soon to be followed by BSE. Then (2000) Foot and Mouth Epidemic. The meat hat reels, as cataclysmic changes threaten to affect its shape almost daily. The purity of its whiteness is now obviously tarnished. But – much like a bride in a whorehouse – it remains jaunty and defiant.

Cadmium, forms felt. Cadmium, incidentally is the 'secret' ingredient that makes Cadbury's chocolate so delicious! I'll bet you didn't know that. Did you know that Osmium is the reason bathtub toys squeak? Or that Oxygen wasn't discovered until 1774, which meant before that people had to breathe Neon? It's true. The Oxygen Conversion Movement was one of the great scientific undertakings of the eighteenth century. It took twenty-five years to complete and there are a few remote pockets of the planet where people still breathe Neon. Most of these folks live in Borneo and are the only people visible at night from outer space. You can learn a lot from reading the Periodic Charts, but you've got to read between the lines.

The elements that really bug me are the redundant ones like Iron and Lead, which are essentially the same thing, as anyone who has ever been hit on the head by a length of pipe will attest to. Iridium and Strontium are also *exactly* the same thing, save for the fact that Iridium smells a little like almonds, which is why it's sometimes used as a garnish. But really, what's the difference?

Then there's Molybdenum. Vile, putrid Molybdenum. The very thought of it makes me want to retch. I can't describe to you how much misery Molybdenum has created in my life. It broke up my fourth marriage, but I don't even want to go into that. It also got into the wall space of my flat a few years back and I thought I was going to have to move out of the place. First of all, it's one of the noisiest elements going. (If you've never heard it, well here's the best description I can think of: it sounds like Manganese but, I don't know, *growlier*.) The neighbours, of course, misdiagnosed it. 'Sounds like you've got Manganese in the walls,' they clucked, but when I called the guy from Manganese-

No-Mor out for a visit, he got in there with a torch and his face turned ashen and he tried to downplay it in that particularly British way. 'Looks like you've got some Molybdenum bits in there,' he said. Being fairly new to the UK at the time, I found the word 'bits' to be slightly disconcerting and way too *not specific enough*! It has been my observation that the British grouping of all things finite can be basically broken down into two distinct categories:

A. Those things that are absolute, definable, categorisable and understood.
B. 'Bits'

In other words, whatever can't be specifically described, are 'bits', and Brits have no qualms about incorporating the word into the most erudite of discussions. Take, for example, this excerpt from *Theories of Quantum Isotopic Oscillation* by Dr Rudolph Naitinger (University of Edinburgh Press, 1999):

. . . the magnetic resonance of the particle is achieved by bombarding the nuclei with a heavy electron. The charged electron then forms an isotope which, upon colliding with some crunchy bits of some kind or another, creates fusion . . .

Whoa! What does he mean by 'crunchy bits'? Quarks? Neutrinos? As a Yank, this term leaves me baffled, although I have to assume every physicist in Britain knows what the hell Dr Naitinger is talking about.

Another example: several weeks ago I was in a London hospital recovering from a small emergency operation. I won't involve you with the details but it involved a fracas with a colour-blind Korean manicurist over some North Atlantic shipping forecasts. Enough said. Anyway the hospital was way overcrowded so the only place they could put me in for post-op recovery was the gift shop. I was lying there on a cot underneath some *South Park* postcards when a couple of trauma-ward surgeons came in to buy cigarettes. Apparently, they were discussing the day's workload:

'Who's in four?'

'Male. Thirtyish. Pub brawler.'

'What's he got?'

'Cerebral haematoma, multiple contusions, infarctions. Also some stabby bits.'

Now, I don't know what the hell haematomas and infarctions are, but I pretty much get the gist of 'stabby bits'. Wonderful how the British can appropriate a whole new set of linguistics by merely adding 'y' to a verb, thus providing a most succinct description. Thus a restaurant full of activity is 'buzzy'. An overly powerful toilet is 'flushy'. Not only is this a judicious use of wording, but it also points out a fundamental difference between Brits and Americans. If an American, for instance, entered a room full of minks he would probably exclaim something like, 'Holy fucking Toledo, this goddamned room is crawling with . . . critters! What the hell is going on? Someone call security!' Whereas a Brit would simply observe, 'My, it's minky in here.'

See what I mean? Anyway, back to my Molybdenumy wallspace. I tried everything to contain it: Santeria, Bahamian Voodoo, nothing worked. You see Molybdenum, due to its isotopic intensity, adds protons at an exponential rate, and if you don't nip it in the bud right away, it will consume your house in a matter of days, encrusting it in a black residue not unlike the stuff that forms around the rim of a ketchup bottle (which is a crude petroleum called Tomato Carbon).

Eventually, a prayer to St Martin-in-the-Fields, the Patron Saint of backing vocals, removed the pestilence from within my walls, but man o' man, I was still sweeping up Molybdenum 'bits' for months afterwards.

glass jaw

January, 2002

S EVERAL DAYS AGO I wandered into a hotel lobby near
Times Square in New York, looking for a public toilet.
By accident, I ended up at the press conference for the
Mike Tyson–Lennox Lewis fight, which at the time was
scheduled for April, 2002. As you may have witnessed on
television, the conference turned into a fiasco. Tyson
attacked Lewis and bit a sizable chunk out of his leg. Later
the Nevada State Boxing Commission would refuse to
grant Tyson permission to fight. As I said, I was there by
accident. Like Sugar Ray Leonard's retina, I am fairly
detached when it comes to boxing. As far as I'm concerned,
the sport is run by morons – morons with brain damage.
Don King acts as if he's brain damaged. Muhammad Ali
is brain damaged. Mike Tyson is a psychopath. If boxing
doesn't cause brain damage, how come they call it a *ring*

when, clearly, it's a *square*? See there? Spatial perception goes right out the window with the first good shot to the head. And don't give me that business about boxing being 'The Gentleman's Sport' or the 'Sport of Kings'. If it's such a manly endeavour, why are they fighting for a belt and a purse? Women *shop* for that stuff.

Leaving the press conference, I strolled out into the gleaming new hotel foyer to take in the view and promptly walked into a plate-glass window. I went down and almost passed out. Lying there woozily, I was aware of a gaggle of concerned passersby materialising over me. One of them, it turns out, was Bob Lee, President of the World Boxing Organisation (one of the roughly 1,376 legitimately recognised boxing title organisations).

'You okay there, Scrumpy Jack?' he asked, helping me up.

'Almost knocked myself out,' I said, feebly. I thanked him and slinked away sheepishly. It was the fourth time in my life I'd walked into a plate-glass window, which is nothing to be proud of, so you can imagine my surprise when last week a friend (and fight fan) of mine telephoned me to inform me that I was now the tenth ranked Light Heavyweight fighter in the world – according to the World Boxing Organisation. I tried to contact the WBO but no one answered.

Then I rang *FightNews*, a leading fight publication, and informed the chief editor that my surprise inclusion in the rankings was obviously a mistake that could happen to anyone. The editor checked his stats and replied no, it was true. He broke it down as follows:

Roy Jones Jr, the WBC and WBA-recognised champion, has, on several occasions, walked into a plate-glass window, but has never knocked himself out. Dariusz Michalczewski, the WBO-recognised champion, has knocked himself out from a plate-glass window only once, but it was double-reinforced and the WBO believes that it probably would have knocked out Roy Jones Jr, given the opportunity.

Clinton Woods, the second ranked Light Heavyweight, has been knocked out once by a plate-glass window. And every other Light Heavyweight in the entire WBA-WBC-IBF-WBO-*FightNews* supercluster has been knocked out *at least twice* by a plate-glass window. Roy Jones Jr's accomplishments aside, my unknocked-out status against plate-glass windows is the most impressive feat of the last few anaemic years of boxing. Thus I was anointed with the ranking.

The editor also informed me I was scheduled to fight a man named Glencoffe Johnson in May in Atlantic City, New Jersey. Glencoffe is the ninth ranked Light Heavyweight Boxer in the WBO. My guaranteed take from the fight, even if I lost, was $1.2 million.

When I received this news I was, by degrees, startled, elated, then paralysed with fear. I'm not ready to die. I need to go up against some perspex or a stack of glass blocks before I can even *think* about fighting Glencoffe Johnson, whom I understand is a pretty intimidating fellow. Friends said, 'Rich, just go in there, let the guy deck you, take the money and run.' Run where? In the Special Olympics? What's the point of being a millionaire if I'm going to drool for the rest of my life?

I telephoned my manager, Addison Cresswell. He was no help.

'You should definitely do it,' he said. I reminded him his milieu was show business. This wouldn't be a corporate gig or a weekend at The Chuckle Hutch. This would be a man trying to kill me.

'Yeah, but it's going to be televised. Three words: Exposure.'

FightNews.com World Boxing Rankings

Return to Fightnews

Due to many requests...

FIGHTNEWS.COM
P4P RATINGS
Click here

Updated January 26, 2002

Heavyweight (unlimited)

WBC	WBA	IBF	WBO	FIGHTNEWS
Lennox Lewis	**John Ruiz**	**Lennox Lewis**	**Wladimir Klitschko**	**1. Lennox Lewis**
1. Mike Tyson	1. Kirk Johnson	1. Chris Byrd	1. Frez Oquendo	2. Wladimir Klitschko
2. Vitali Klitschko	2. Evander Holyfield	2. Not rated	2. Vitali Klitschko	3. Mike Tyson
3. Hasim Rahman	3. Vitaly Klitschko	3. Fres Oquendo	3. Jameel McCline	4. Chris Byrd
4. Fres Oquendo	4. Mike Tyson	4. Hasim Rahman	4. Chris Byrd	5. Fres Oquendo
5. Oliver McCall	5. Fres Oquendo	5. Kirk Johnson	5. Kirk Johnson	6. Kirk Johnson
6. Kirk Johnson	6. Nicolay Valuev	6. Jameel McCline	6. David Tua	7. Vitali Klitschko
7. Chris Byrd	7. Oliver McCall	7. Monte Barrett	7. Danny Williams	8. Hasim Rahman
8. Vaughn Bean	8. Jameel McCline	8. Ray Mercer	8. Oliver McCall	9. Evander Holyfield
9. Larry Donald	9. Larry Donald	9. David Tua	9. Luan Krasniqi	10. John Ruiz
10. Michael Moorer	10. Hasim Rahman	10. Oliver McCall	10. Lance Whitaker	11. Jameel McCline
				12. David Tua

Cruiserweight (190 lbs)

WBC	WBA	IBF	WBO	FIGHTNEWS
Juan Carlos Gomez	**Virgil Hill**	**Vassily Jirov**	**Johnny Nelson**	**1. Vassily Jirov**
1. Wayne Braithwaite	1. Jean Marc Mormeck	1. Jorge Castro	1. Vincenzo Cantatore	2. Juan Carlos Gomez
2. Vincenzo Cantatore	2. Alexander Gurov	2. Not Rated	2. Alexander Gurov	3. Virgil Hill
3. O'Neil Bell	3. James Toney	3. O'Neil Bell	3. Wayne Braithwaite	4. James Toney
4. Alexander Gurov	4. Wayne Braithwaite	4. Alexander Gurov	4. O'Neil Bell	5. Johnny Nelson
5. Carlos Cruzat	5. Fabrice Tiozzo	5. James Toney	5. Dale Brown	6. O'Neil Bell
6. Louis Azille	6. O'Neil Bell	6. Wayne Braithwaite	6. Ramon Garbey	7. Wayne Braithwaite
7. Dale Brown	7. Ezra Sellers	7. Arthur Williams	7. Jorge Castro	8. Alexander Gurov
8. Sebsatian Rothman	8. Vincenzo Cantatore	8. Fabrice Tiozzo	8. James Toney	9. Ezra Sellers
9. Bruce Scott	9. Luis Pineda	9. Ezra Sellers	9. Ezra Sellers	10. Fabrice Tiozzo
10. Arthur Williams	10. Jorge Castro	10. Imamu Mayfield	10. Louis Azille	11. Jorge Castro
				12. Jean Marc Mormeck

Light Heavyweight (175 lbs)

WBC	WBA	IBF	WBO	FIGHTNEWS
Roy Jones	**Roy Jones**	**Roy Jones**	**Dariusz Michalczewski**	**1. Roy Jones**
1. Clinton Woods	**Bruno Girard**	1. Glen Kelly	1. Clinton Woods	2. D. Michalczeweski
2. Reggie Johnson	1. Lou Del Valle	2. Reggie Johnson	2. Glenn Kelly	3. Antonio Tarver
3. Yawe Davis	2. Glenn KellyNot Rated	3. Eric Harding	3. Eric Harding	4. Eric Harding
4. Antonio Tarver	3. Reggie Johnson	4. Antonio Tarver	4. Antonio Tarver	5. Clinton Woods
5. Mads Larsen	4. Clinton Woods	5. Glencoffe Johnson	5. Jean Marc Mormeck	6. Reggie Johnson
6. Eric Harding	5. Thomas Hansvoll	6. Clinton Woods	6. Alejandro Lakatus	7. Bruno Girard
7. Glenn Kelly	6. David Telesco	7. David Telesco	7. Reggie Johnson	8. Glen Kelly
8. Julio Gonzalez	7. Antonio Tarver	8. Will Taylor	8. David Telesco	9. David Telesco
9. Michael Nunn	8. Mads Larsen	9. Bruno Girard	9. Glencoffe Johnson	10. Montell Griffin
10. Bruno Girard	9. Glencoffe Johnson	10. Lou Del Valle	10. Richard Hall	11. Glencoffe Johnson
	10. Robert Koon			12. Lou Del Valle

Super Middleweight (168 lbs)

102

'I couldn't fight my way out of a paper bag,' I said. Addison hung up. Within minutes he called back.

'I got you a warm-up with a paper bag,' he said. 'Royston Leisure Centre. Same bag that went nine rounds with Frank Bruno.'

'Forget it, Addison,' I said.

But he was tenacious. He devised a strategy – one that has worked for a lot of boxers of late – of creating a hopeless muddle of legal injunctions, title disputes and assorted contractual hang-ups that would effectively maintain my ranking without my ever actually having to *set foot* in the ring. This way I can, at least, milk the exposure and maybe even snag a few product endorsements. Savvy, I had to admit. Addison, working his mumbo-jumbo, has managed to play off the myriad boxing organisations against each other and ultimately my situation stands as follows: I will fight Glencoffe Johnson early next autumn *provided* I can settle my dispute with the WBC, which fails to recognise my standing in the division and in fact, claims to have never even heard of me, *and* provided Dariusz Michalczewski, the number one ranked boxer, first agrees to fight either Alejandro Lakatus, the Bosnian fighter, or the actual country of Bosnia itself, provided Bosnia doesn't first fight Serbia, and provided Serbia comes in at weight. Also I'm not allowed to go near any plate-glass windows.

both guns drawn

THERE'S BEEN A false spring in London for the last week or so and pubgoers have been spilling out on to the pavement like basking seals. Sometimes when I come across these gatherings, it makes me wary and uneasy. As an American, the sight of hordes of people huddled outside a building generally indicates one thing: someone *inside* has a gun. Hardly a day goes by in the Good Ol' US of A when CNN isn't cutting live to an office building or work plant where some miswired winky-doodle has emptied the place out with a semi-automatic while the local swat team attempts to talk him down on all fours. As the 'drama unfolds live', reporters will invariably proffer some armchair psychological profiles from the displaced witnesses. As a rule, the further south these incidents occur the more colourful the accounts. *'I don't know. I think the cheese just slipped kinda off his cracker,'* or, *'I always knew that sonofabitch would pull some stunt like this. Tell ya the truth, I coulda gone all day without this happening.'*

Eventually the guy (it's always a guy – women don't shoot their fellow employees in America) is led out in cuffs. Or he tops himself, or the snipers do him in. Then the town is proclaimed to be 'reeling from shock' and will have to begin a 'painful rebuilding period'. Then the network returns to Larry King snapping his red braces whilst interviewing celebs.

Thus when I see those Londoners milling about outside, I'm relieved to realise, Oh! they're only drinking. There's lots of things not to like about London, but most people seem to be keeping their cheese firmly on top of their crackers.

The question I'm often asked by Brits is, 'Why can't the US change its gun laws?' And believe me, that is a perfectly valid question. Which I can't answer. The answer many Yanks would give you is 'because we needed to arm ourselves 225 years ago when we went to war with Britain and there's *every possibility in the world they may try to pull that shit again.* And if not Britain then, well, you know, Cuba or Iraq or Wales or some crazed Muslim terrorists or maybe black-ops from the CIA in stealth helicopters or, quite possibly the guy in the cubicle next to me who can spout whole chapters from *The Turner Diaries* word for word.'

Furthermore, in America we have several pillars enforcing the right to carry guns. One, of course, is the Constitution. The Constitution guarantees the 'right to bear arms'. Never mind that this was drafted in 1776 when the nation's population was 412 and the 'arms' referred to were flintlock muskets that required roughly thirteen steps to fire:

1. Espy approaching enemy (i.e. British Redcoats)
2. Mutter to oneself, 'Sweet Jumpin' Jesus, here comes a Redcoat Loyalist who's threatening my God-given right to carry this flimsy contraption of forged iron and oak in my hands!'
3. Remove gunpowder from horn of dead elk
4. Check to see powder is dry
5. Pour powder into musket
6. Add bleach and softener
7. Search around for giant lead-weighted musket ball
8. Pack with long-handled wadder
9. Check flint
10. Look up to see that Redcoat is performing the same oafish and cumbersome procedure
11. Aim
12. Fire and scream lustily as powder discharge temporarily blinds you
13. Once sight is regained look around to notice the only thing you've hit is the cow behind you

In other words, in 1776 it was easier to do pioneer algorithms than fire a gun. But today's beady-eyed gunbunnies still stand on that leaky proclamation, claiming it's their legacy to own a .70mm hand howitzer with an infrared scope and armour-piercing bullets.

We also have the incredibly powerful handgun owners lobby who, missing the irony bus, call themselves the National Rifle Association. The NRA's function is to squelch any restrictive gun legislature. They do this by funnelling huge wads of cash into the hands of senators and congressmen, usually meeting them clandestinely in the bleachers of little league baseball games, concealing the money in *Star Wars* lunchpails. This keeps the senator's mind sharp next time a bill comes around suggesting that sixteen-year-olds in camouflage shouldn't be allowed to enter gun shops muttering phrases like 'it's time to thin the herd'.

Bullets are the pop rivets that hold America's sociopath society together. Americans *love* guns. Shooting a gun – and this has been proven – adds inches to one's manhood. In Times Square in New York, there's a gun clock which advances every time an American citizen is killed by a handgun. New Yorkers used to shoot each other in Times Square just to watch the clock change. Of course that was the old New York City. Now there's a seven-day waiting period for gun purchases, presumably to allow hot heads to 'cool off'. It's barely caused a ripple in the American psyche.

Clerk:	Can I help you?
Hothead:	Yes, I'd like to purchase that Taurus .45 in the glass case.
Clerk:	Certainly, sir. Of course there's a seven-day waiting period.
Hothead:	Okay. I'll wait right over here.

This explanation doesn't really hold much truck with Brits, because they don't feel the need to shoot their bosses, since they're not even really sure who their boss is, or if one ever existed. So when Londoners ask me, 'Why is it so easy to acquire a gun in America?' I skilfully deflect the question by asking, 'Why is it so difficult to get a beer in London?' Taking into account the amount of time spent waiting amongst thirsty throngs for a truculent bartender to serve you, factored by the stingy opening hours, I have calculated that the *actual* waiting time for a pint in London is *longer than that for a gun in America*. After all you can buy a handgun in America any hour of the day or night. *Try* to find a beer in London after eleven p.m. You need a gun.

The reason one can't get a beer very easily in England (or so I'm told) is more or less the same as our gun logic. 'Because eighty-five years ago, when we were at war with the Germans, a few nonparticipatory types sneaked down to the pub for a snort when they were *supposed* to be filling bullet casings, and God knows we don't want that to happen again, so we close at eleven sharp in case Germany attacks us again.'

In essence, two of the greatest nations on earth are making life miserable for themselves out of fear of an uprising by a European Nation.

Both laws concern themselves with self-preservation. If gun laws are *too lax* in America and pub laws in Britain are *too harsh*, wouldn't the ideal solution be for the two nations to trade laws? Let Londoners drink whenever they want. But close the gun shops in America early.

Were it impossible to purchase a pistol after eleven p.m. in America, I'm sure murders would be reduced by at least half, since a substantial percentage of Americans get themselves plugged in the wee hours. Gun shops could even be more like pubs. You know, a kind of gathering place for gun enthusiasts; with 'Gun Quiz Nights' and summertime 'garden shootouts'. Beer drinkers tend to congregate. Gun buyers would probably do the same, thus increasing the likelihood they'll shoot each other instead of me.

There's a fuzzy but nonetheless valid conclusion to draw from this. Brits don't – as a rule – shoot each other because a) it's rude and b) can't you see they're busy drinking? If America had a pub on every corner instead of a gun dealer, it might find itself becoming a more live-able country, literally. If you're going to end up on the floor with a dozen shots in you, better it be vodka than bullets, right?

saving bryan adams

I T WAS IN February of this year that the US Military, financially strapped, opened its doors to corporate sponsorship. Naturally, Britain and other stalwarts of capitalism followed suit. It couldn't have come at a better time. Not only did the infusion of much-needed cash shore up the dwindling resources of the Free World's fighting forces, it gave soldiers a morale boost. Stranded thousands of miles from home, they merely needed to gaze down at the shiny KFC logo plastered across their chest to relieve any wistful pangs of homesickness.

I was conscripted in early March. President Bush was itching to find a new enemy. Having finally defeated Terrorism, he was considering a war on some other Evil . . . Rudeness perhaps. Or Unsanitary Food Preparation. Suddenly, a viable target reared its ugly serpent's head: the tiny African nation of Burkina Faso was found to be trafficking in pirated cds.

A US spy drone (The FujiFilm Reconnaissance Blimp)

had secretly photographed a huge truckload of counterfeit cds being transported from a makeshift factory in Ouagadougou to a port in Liberia, where they were to be loaded on to a freighter bound for North Korea. It was now abundantly clear that Burkina Faso was flaunting its illegal trade in what Bush called 'Intellectual Property' and the rest of us called 'Crap Kylie Minogue Albums'.

Standing alongside special envoy Bono, Bush addressed a hastily assembled press corps. 'This is not about oppression or human injustice,' he snapped, exuding all the bluster of a chihuahua who thinks it's a terrier. 'This is about protecting America's artistic purity. Our Constitution guarantees the Kylie Minogues and Janet Jacksons of the world their due royalties and once North Korea gets a listening of the Gypsy Kings, they'll be a fulcrum in the Axis of Easy Listening. If blood must be spilled to stop this, then hot-diggety-damn, it's Go-Time, people!'

Since the bulk of America's troops were bogged down in the Caribbean, trying to intercept six Cuban dissidents, who were attempting to cross the sea by toilet seat with garden strimmers for outboard motors, in order to blow up a crab shack in Key Largo, Florida, a call-up had been organised. At the time, I was a lifelong member of the Columbia Record Club, so I was in the first wave of conscripts. I remember getting the form letter. Basically, it said I had a choice: purchase fifty cds at the club price of $14.99 each or else report for active duty to Camp Pizza Hut at Fort Riley, Kansas. I don't have to tell you which choice I made. The thought of some infidel peddling bogus Springsteen made my red American blood boll. I packed my duffel and told the wife if I didn't make it back, she could have my stereo.

I was assigned to the Columbia Popular Artists Division. Our job was to protect everything from early Dylan to Streisand. Also the more obscure stuff, like Leonard Cohen. We were taught how to spot Xeroxed sleeve liners, substandard jewel cases, substandard Jewel albums, muddied backing tracks – all the telltale signs of piracy. Also how to kill people. I must've memorised a thousand album covers. I could recognise 'em blind-folded.

On 27 May my battalion boarded the USS *Playstation II* and set off across the Atlantic for Monrovia, Liberia. Our objective was clear: to cut off the major supply route for the cd counterfeiters and to make our presence known. After four days at sea, we deployed D-SNIBs (Doritos Super Nacho Inflatable Boats) and silently established a beachhead at Monrovia Harbour. There we were met by the 15th Bud Light Infantry Brigade (BLIB) who had already pushed past their forward operating base at Camp Pennzoil to prevent any pirates from approaching the docked freighter.

Two platoons of FARTHUMMERS (Firestone All-Radial Tyre Humvees) mounted with automatic grenade launchers, .50 calibre heavy machine guns and Mr Whippy Missile Systems ran interference for us, as we pushed east to monitor traffic entering the town. Everyone was jumpy. Earlier that afternoon, two sentries from Britain's SBS (Specialbrew Boat Service) had been ambushed when they tried to intercept a small utility vehicle carrying fifty counterfeit Frank Zappa albums. We'd been briefed on arriving that the enemy had amassed a huge stockpile of Mick Jagger's new album (the real thing, apparently, not counterfeits), and were at this very moment prepared to launch the album.

Twenty minutes into the mission we got reports of a

heavily laden transport vehicle headed straight for us. British Royal Marine scouts from the SCFC/KFC/ MPFC/SCAT (Sebastian Coe Fitness Centres/Kentucky Fried Chicken/Mrs Paul's Fish & Chips/Special Combined Anti-Armour Team) stretched a 10-metre coil of concertina wire across the narrow macadamised road. Chemlights were attached to the wire to make it visible to drivers, giving them fair warning to turn back.

The scouts crouched back a few metres from the road and waited, their Oil of Olay .50-calibre sniper rifles poised. We were about fifty metres away, ready for backup. The air was oppressive and sweltering. My Mr Jacket Potato Flak Jacket hung on me like a lead blanket. But I wasn't about to take it off.

What happened next took us all by surprise. Just as the truck approached, from nowhere, a Charlie Parker cd screeched through the darkness and landed right in our midst. We all dove for cover. It was 'Round Midnight. No one had expected the Pirates to be into jazz. A few hours later came a withering volley of early Simon & Garfunkel. It was wednesday morning three a.m. That's when all hell broke loose. They hit us with Everything But The Girl. I saw a sudden whizzing silvery flash of plastic and felt something tear into my leg, but I didn't pay much attention to it. There's just too much music these days.

We dug in and waited for the enemy to exhaust their back-catalogue. Then we went on the offensive. The ground shook and the sky glowed as F-14 Manny's House Of Waterbeds Fighter Jets dropped 10,000 pound bombs, as well as some coupons for SlimFast, on to the vehicular target. Afterwards nothing moved. It was over that fast.

The number of casualties we inflicted wasn't significant. But the message was: no one was going to interfere with the Free Western World's God-given right to crisp, clear production values. Trudging back to our base, I felt a warm surge of pride coursing through my veins. And the sense of a job well done. It was only then that I looked to see the shrapnel – a silvery shard of John Mellencamp cd – protruding from my calf. And let me tell you, mister – It Hurt So Good.

water chestnuts

L AST WEEK I bought a Mars bar at my local newsagents. Strolling along, I unwrapped it and sunk my molars in. It was old, white and brittle. I took it back to the newsagent.

'This Mars bar is old,' I said.

'Whaddya mean?' the newsagent grunted.

'I mean it's turned to guano,' I replied

'Take another one,' he said and went back to shelving copies of *TeeHee: The Magazine of Filipino Girls who Like to be Tickled.*

I did. It was as old and tasteless as the Dead Sea Scrolls. (Don't ask me how I know what a Dead Sea Scroll tastes like. It's a long story and I've apologised to the Essenes.) Anyway, I asked for my money back. The newsagent refused. At this point a small, very testy queue had formed behind me like vultures on a fence rail. Several people were flinging loose coins my way. So I gave up the standoff.

Once outside, I noticed on the offending Mars wrapper a small explanatory banner:

MAKE IT HAPPEN! A WINNER A DAY UNTIL 2000!

Apparently Mars was sponsoring a promotion to make people's 'dreams come true'.
'Have a single released. Be in a soap opera. Send your granny bungee jumping. Train with NASA. Drive a car around Monaco! Tell us [what you want] and we could make it happen for you. Send us a 30-word entry . . .'
Lemme see if I have this straight . . . The folks at Mars can train astronauts and jaunt people around Monaco but I can't get my money back on a two-year-old calcified chocolate bar? Unless of course I write a thirty-word entry to the company professing that a refund had been my lifelong dream.

How can Mars afford to train NASA astronauts? Are they taking their name a little too seriousy? Or is NASA *that* desperate for astronauts? I was fairly astounded by the magnanimity of this gesture, so much so that I went back to the newsagents to see what other swag Britain's snack industry is dangling in front of buyers. Well, Sir, a quick survey of the shelves revealed that Twiglets is giving away a million pounds. Mars Milk Chocolate Drink is giving away £30,000 of 'Street Gear'. (Whatever *that* means. Maybe it's just some automotive parts they found lying in the road.) And Galaxy Fruit and Nut bars is giving away 'Home Makeovers'. Now that *is* a dream come true . . . having your home redecorated by Chocolate Workers. I'll bet they know their way around the earth tones. Looks like the nibbles retailers are well into averages and rewarding their customers handsomely. Keep snacking Britain!

Then I went into Sainsbury's. It was a Jetsetters' clearinghouse. Maltissimo Mocha Powder, for instance, was offering to send lucky winners to Milan, Rome and Venice. That's gotta be their entire profit margin for the year because frankly I don't know one person who's ever purchased Maltissimo Mocha Powder. Blue Valley Water Chestnuts was 'proudly' offering a flight to the 'Holiday Destination of your Choice'. When was the last time you – or anyone you know – bought water chestnuts?! I'm willing to bet the next person who *buys* a can of Blue Valley Water Chestnuts can just take his bags down to Sainsbury's, plop down for a can of water chestnuts, then head for the nearest Concorde.

My favourite was the Pal Dog Food Promotion. There, on the label of the can containing high-quality, prime animal eyeballs and snouts was a small banner exclaiming 'Win two Peugeots'! In view of the recent foot and mouth outbreak, it's good to see there's no animosity (hey, hey!!) between the French and British as far as the pet food trade is concerned. My question is: how come this promotion is rewarding humans and not the dogs who actually have to *eat the stuff*? Pal clearly hasn't thought this through. They should be offering a lucky dog entrant two Peugeot tyres.

It went on. Shelf after shelf of untapped wealth and consumer largesse. Some of the giveaways were nothing more than trinkets, but curious nonetheless. Nêstlés, for instance, was giving away *Reader's Digest* subscriptions to purchasers of Fibre 1 cereal. Fair enough. Obviously a campaign targeted for its geriatric buying public. But another Nêstlés' cereal, Shreddies, was offering *A Bug's Life* magnifying glasses. Why shouldn't the old people be eligible for those as well? It could help them to read the *Reader's Digest*. (Nêstlés wasn't offering large-type

joo-joo eyeball

IT'S PROBABLY HAPPENED to you a few times. You're strolling up the high street, minding your own beeswax, when suddenly some full-blown nutcake approaches, pie-eyed and babbling, his brain commandeered by unseen demons.

'Stalin's yes-man!! Seldom drunk before the afternoon!' he screams, desperate and incomprehensible. You try to sidestep him, but he's agile. 'Help me, please. Stalin's yes man . . . !!!'

You don't know what to do about this fruitbat. You try to give him some money. He flings it away.

Actually the correct action would be to say, 'Molotov Cocktail'. Why? Because he's looking for the answer to a cryptic crossword clue.

I used to think all these people shuffling around town screaming incoherently at strangers were what my grandma used to call 'full-blown winkies'. But that was before I started working cryptic crosswords in this

121

country. Now I realise many of these nutters are strung out from trying to crack the things. I have never encountered anything more addled or tortuous than British crosswords. Unlike their American counterparts – *The New York Times* crossword puzzle, for example – which offer clever, diversionary clues that jog one's latent knowledge, cryptic crosswords are apparently designed by dyslexic idiot savants who have read Everything Ever Written but never learned to diagram a sentence. *The New York Times* crossword is a delicate latticework of words, dovetailing into each other: an ingeniously constructed City of Language. In cryptic crosswords the words don't even *talk* to their neighbours! In American puzzles, if you can fill in, say, 14 down, well, *that* word will become your friend and merrily assist you in solving both 14 across and 17 down, and soon the whole puzzle begins to unfold, flowering to a glorious and satisfying finale. Cryptic crosswords are selfish, quarantined bastards. They have all the logic of London street planning. Where's the momentum? If, after four hours of furious brain flagellation, scrawling out insane graffiti around the corners of the puzzle, chewing your fingernails and generally setting aside all personal and civic responsibilities in your life, you *do* manage to complete a blank, well, where does that leave you? Nowhere! You have to start all over again with a new clue, like a detective who keeps getting moved to a new case. And you wonder why Brits have consigned themselves to a diet of disappointment.

I suppose this goes a long way toward illustrating how Yanks and Brits differ in their thought processes. Americans, generally speaking, are linear thinkers. Americans invented the assembly line. And the buffet line, come to think of it. Thus, a typical American crossword clue looks like this:

Clue: HOST OF '92 SUMMER GAMES
Answer: BARCELONA

See there? Simple, isn't it? Compare that to this convoluted British witterance:

Clue: FORMER SRI LANKAN KICKS OUT FEMALE
CHROMOSOME INSIDE BACKWARD SAUDI TYPE.
SPANISH TWIST. CRAB ALONE! (9)

Whaaaaaaat? It's just a puzzle for cryinoutloud, not the Enigma code. Why does every clue have to sound like Poetry Slam Night at the Java Hutch? My systematic approach to problem solving precludes me from ever completing a single blank of these infernal things, and makes me want to stab the dog with a pencil. Who can fathom these arcane, mind-boggling clues:

Across:

1.   APPLAUSE SPILLS FORTH FROM JOWLS OF
      OAKEN BADMINTON INSECT (2)
5.   WHAT THE DENTIST SAID WHEN THE SEA
      CAPTAIN RUBBED HIS NOODLES (3,4,93)

Down:

3.   SOME SQUIRRELS DO THIS WHEN (See 12
      across) EASTER ARRIVES AND THERE ARE
      NO RADISHES (see 17 down) AND RUFUS
      ATE THE PLASTIC CHUNKS (See 3 across
      from last Wednesday's puzzle) (6)

In fact, I have always suspected that the lyrics to the

Beatles song 'Come Together' is nothing more than John Lennon reciting clues from that particular morning's cryptic crossword:

Across:

6. HERE COME OLD FLAT TOP, HE COME
    GROOVING UP SLOWLY (12)
7. HE GOT JOO-JOO EYEBALL (5,7)
8. HE ONE HOLY ROLLER (3,4,6)

The answers are, of course (6) Butterscotch (7) Marty Feldman and (7) One Holy Roller.

I've always considered crossword-solving to be a waste of valuable intellect. If you can figure these things out, why aren't you calculating Pi, or solving the algorithm that bends the time–space continuum? I detest that smug, self-satisfied look people get on their faces after they've completed a puzzle. My, my, my, aren't you a caution? In fact, I've devised a pleasant little revenge for these hollow victors. Buy yourself one of those Super Cryptic Egghead Level Puzzle Mags, photocopy a puzzle from it, memorise the answers (listed in the back) and carry it with you at all times. Then, when you're on a train with Mr Crossword genius, slaving over his own puzzle, casually whip out your Puzzle Extraordinaire and smarmily breeze through it at supersonic speed. Watch as his eyes keep darting nervously toward your handiwork, his face getting angrier, sweatier, more intimidated, until eventually he collapses under the weight of his own inferiority and shuffles off at his stop, a sad, defeated lump of protoplasm, presumably, with any luck, hurling himself on to the tracks and snuffing out his useless life.

vinegar and verse

T HE POETRY WORLD mourns the passing this week of the estimable C. Pervis Shanks (1920–2002), Britain's near poet-laureate and lifelong contributor to the *Loughborough University Poetry Review*. That Mr Shanks never achieved the status of his illustrious cohorts T.S. Eliot, Samuel Beckett or Anne Sexton is a fairly criminal oversight on the part of critics and scholars alike. He was revered in literary circles by all as a gentle visionary – a man who in his own words envisioned 'a dandelion world through raw walrus eyes'. T.S. Eliot once said of C. Pervis Shanks, 'a more rarefied fellow I've yet to meet. Shanks has seen a few things and it is to our credit he chooses to share them with us. Also, he has my lawn mower. Ah well! He will return it in his own sweet time.'

Mr Shanks' response to this elegiac remark was through his usual medium – a poem. His 'Ode to a Mower Borrow'd' contained some brutal and unforgettable imagery.

In bitter weeds, this June hath chosen
Lies your mower, axle frozen

Sadly, Shanks' work was all too often overlooked. Shanks was short-listed by the Nobel Prize Committee – only to lose – so many times he began to believe it was a personal grudge. Accolades and near misses did nothing to boost his sense of self-worth. For Shanks was, by his own admission, a lifelong defeated wordsmith. 'I am sick of the vinegar of my verse', he writes in 'The Bile Foundry' (1958):

Its puerile waft, its rancid vapour
Oh *smite* this rancour
Oh *smelt* this bitter ore
Oh *smoot* this empty idyll
This apologetic wheeze of my own hollow breath

Indeed, 'The Bile Foundry' deftly illustrates how a typically brilliant Shanks poem can be undermined by a single baffling line – this particular example being 'Oh *smoot* this empty idyll'. Nowhere in any known language does the word 'smoot' exist. Advised of this by his peers, Shanks remained intractable. His editor/agent at the time, William C. Felker, casually suggested supplanting 'smoot' with 'smash', 'squash' or perhaps even 'squelch'. But Shanks became extremely irate and attacked Felker about the neck and shoulders with a small uncooked partridge, which he carried with him for just such outbursts.

'Shanks was an arsehole,' recalls Felker, in a less than poignant evaluation. Asked to elaborate he adds, 'All right, he was a prick as well. I admired the man but there's no excuse for his behaviour. There's no such word

126

as "smoot". End of story. To this day I can't lift my right arm above my shoulder.'

I reminded Mr Felker that all artists can be extremely passionate about criticism, that a proclivity for unpredictable violence wasn't unusual amongst creative artists. 'Look at Jackson Pollock,' I said.

'Where?' replied Felker, looking around.

I added that it was an artist's prerogative to invent words. '. . . sleep that ravels up the knitted sleeve of care,' I said, quoting Shakespeare. 'What does "ravel" mean? It's not an antonym of "unravel", is it?'

Felker thought about this momentarily, then, in what seemed like a small concession, answered, 'Come to think of it, maybe it was a squab, not a partridge.'

As is so often the case, C. Pervis Shanks seemed his own worst enemy. His legendary bouts with alcohol made for eye-opening dinner-party stories, but tragically hindered his artistic momentum. For example, his entire literary output from 1959 until 1977 consisted of the following rather obtuse sonnet:

BIBBILY BOOBLY

Bibbily boobly bobble blib blib
Blibbery blubbery blob-blooble
Boogety boogety boo!

Convinced (in his less than lucid condition) that the poem had theatrical merits, Shanks attempted to mount 'Bibbily Boobly' as a dramatic reading. He sought the assistance of Tony Marsden, who had just staged an outstanding, successful production of Dylan Thomas's *Under Milkwood* at the Regents Theatre in London's

West End. Marsden tried to convince Shanks the reading would be a fiasco, but Shanks, as usual, wouldn't listen.

'"Bibbily Boobly" is a nova!' he pleaded with Marsden. 'It blazes across the indigo night and – lest mankind miss it – I shall, if only for a moment, immortalise it on stage!'

'I pointed out that the word he was probably looking for was "comet", as novas are generally stationary,' recalls Marsden. 'Then, observing how pissed he was, I rather unwisely suggested he should call the reading "Imbibbily Boob", at which point C. Pervis began threatening me with that goddamned partridge he was always carrying around.'

Marsden forcibly entered Shanks into a recovery programme, which probably saved his life. He emerged in 1981 with his most electrifying work yet, the astonishing 'Colours of My Hell'. With terse, vivid imagery Shanks chronicles his descent into alcoholism:

> Beryl Green, Evergreen, Sea vale
> Citron, Tawny Golden, Autumn fields
> Buttercup and Bronze
> Fiery Red! Matador Red! Fierce Red!
> Crimson! Burnt Crimson!
> . . . Black
> Mud Black
> Infinite Black

It was a poem of such visceral starkness that it rocked the poetry world and nailed shut forever the coffin lid of criticism. Shanks won the 1982 Nobel Prize for Poetry, hands down. Sadly, it was withdrawn upon discovery that the entire poem consisted of the names of interior paint samples Shanks had chanced upon at a hardware store.

Crushed and humiliated, Shanks spent the remainder of his life a recluse, puttering about his garden, shooing away the occasional partridge-sniffing cat. He will be missed.

the mile high club

W ITH MARGARET YOU just never knew where you
stood. It always seemed to Wayman Barksdale that
he would eventually cheat on her, and when he did it
wasn't recklessly, but with a kind of glum certitude that
things may never get better at home, so what the hell.
He was on a personal roll at the time, rocketing into the
public eye with a low entry on to the bestseller list, a
guest spot on the *Oprah Winfrey Show* in Chicago, and
a round trip BA ticket from London.

'Notice we haven't made love in a while?' he said to her
the evening before he was supposed to leave for America.
He tried to make it sound offhand, the way you might
say, 'Notice you don't hear much from Barry Manilow
anymore?'
    'What would be the point of that?' Margaret replied.
    They had a map of Chicago opened on the dining-room
table and he was studying the layout of the town. To

Wayman, a transplanted American, it was going to be good to get back for a while: Polish sausages and corner taverns, midwestern how-do-you-do. To her it was just a spot on the map. All the implicit encouragement she had given him through his early attempts at writing now seemed to have evaporated. Maybe she was just jealous. She was a writer too, a serious one. Wayman's novel wasn't exactly Booker prize material. It was about a London madame who threatens to reveal the names of her celebrity clients unless she gets a larynx transplant. It was called *The Whore Whisperer.* He'd received a million pound advance. The final instalment had arrived earlier that day.

Wayman himself viewed professional jealousy as direly self-defeating. He tried to explain that to Margaret.

'Remember that poem "Richard Cory"?' he said to her.

'Who?'

'The one about the guy who had everything and then . . . one day Richard Cory "went home and put a bullet in his head".'

'What's your point?'

'It's about the ephemerality of fortune.'

Wayman rummaged through his poetry anthologies and found the poem. Margaret read it.

'This *is* a remarkable poem,' she said, trying to sound contrite. 'It makes me appreciate the fact that even though I don't make much money, I probably make more than the fuckwit who wrote this, so he can kiss my arse.'

He just didn't know where he stood.

On the plane to Chicago he met a very pretty flight attendant. He had been avoiding her chirpy attempts to serve him an amorphous entrée. He kept his head bowed intently over itinerary faxes. She reappeared with a chemical-dipped face towel, leaning a bit closer to him than the trained distance. Her name tag read 'Gwendolyn'.

'Are you okay?'

'Never better.'

'Sure I can't get you something to eat?'

'No thanks.'

The towels had that nauseating punge that Asians seem to like and everyone else finds nauseating.

'Saw you on *Richard and Judy*, talking about your book. It was good.'

'Thanks for watching.'

Then, out of the blue, she put her lips to his ear and said, 'Wanna join the Mile High Club?'

Wayman wasn't sure he'd heard her right. Maybe what she had asked was 'Do you enjoy mild Ohio gloves?' He was considering an answer to Question B when she said it again.

'You know . . . the Mile High Club?' This time she winked and indicated the washroom.

'Meet you in there in a jiff,' she said, squeezing his hand, resonating the kind of hospitality he hadn't seen on a British Airways flight in quite a long time.

He got up, shuffled up the aisle, a bit speciously, and squeezed himself into the washroom. He studied himself in the mirror. It seemed important to get a good picture of a man about to embark on a period of 'womanising'. The question of his ropy status with Margaret was still there, as incessant as the drone of the aeroplane, but he just didn't know what to do about it. He looked around the tiny cubicle at all the pictoglyphs with their stern Teutonic warnings. If anything went wrong in here it could force an emergency landing.

Then the door opened and there was some painful negotiation as he tried not to be killed accordion-style. Gwendolyn wedged herself in and locked the bolt behind her. She quickly began divesting herself of her corporate get-up.

'What I liked about you,' she said, unbuttoning her blouse, 'is that you seemed so *absorbed* . . .' Then the blouse was in his face. It looked like a proof sheet of Union Jacks. '. . . but nice. Famous people are so up their own arses.'

'Would you be here if you hadn't seen me on TV?' he asked.

'Well, to tell you the truth, *I* didn't see you on the TV. But one of the other staff did.'

Wayman couldn't quite make himself trust the sunniness of this escapade. But Gwendolyn had an airy assurance that kind of just made him want to ride the thermals for a while.

'I'm not much of a reader,' she said, tugging at his shirt. 'Adventure mags, I suppose. Got a danger streak in me this wide. Undo your belt.'

'Righto. Lemme just get my shirt off first . . .' He was wearing a Harley-Davidson t-shirt underneath.

'Well now, do you own one of these?'

'Yeah,' Wayman replied, curtly as possible. To him any discussion of Harley's at the cosmetic level smacked of cheap machismo. Also, he was anxious to see if it was possible to actually get laid in a thirty-four square cubic centimetre space. This whole Mile High Club business was more of a gymnastic feat than any real heartfelt exchange of emotion, he concluded.

'I *luuuuuuuuv* Harleys . . .' she was saying, extending the word into a tigery phonetic. Her chattiness was beginning to annoy him. He felt a low, mordant atmosphere best suited his impending moral pivot, but in this overlit sarcophagus, it wasn't remotely sexy. Her face, now suddenly close to his was tilted at a skewy angle, like a sunflower. Deftly she tried to remove her brassiere and caught him with an elbow uppercut. A whorl of talcum powder and moisturiser smells ascended from her bare torso and almost made him choke. His attempt to get his trousers off was waylaid by a burst of air turbulence and as the plane momentarily plummeted, he found his mouth on hers, even as he was trying to coax a trouser leg over a shoe heel. Eventually, with her perched precipitously on the sink ledge, he was able to achieve some marginal degree of penetration, but it owed more to the plane's forward thrust than his own. It took another ten minutes to get their clothes back on. All the while someone was tapping on the outside door.

Afterwards, as Wayman headed back to his seat, a number of passengers gave him a knowing, lecherous smile. He sunk into his seat and watched the eastern seaboard of America pass beneath, the gallerias and baseball diamonds pinned to the hazy landscape like badges. You could see that America was just a fat man joining two oceans, whose Elvis belt buckle was Chicago. Exiting the plane, he passed Gwendolyn mouthing 'bub-eye' robotically to departing passengers.

'Have a safe time in Chicago, Mister Man . . .' she chirruped at him, then winked. 'And welcome to the Mile High Club.'

He smiled back, sheepishly. Already, the guilt was kicking in.

He chatted up his book to Oprah, who called it 'sizzling', 'crackling good', and 'so hot it burned her fingers'. It occurred to Wayman these were all things you could say about sausages. He drove back to his hotel in a rental car. In the lobby he drank Rolling Rock from the bottle while people around him talked at a volume Brits use only to call their children in. It was Cubs this and Stock Exchange that. At about six p.m. he went upstairs and phoned Margaret in London. There was no answer. He felt quite relentlessly guilty.

Three days after he arrived back home in London, the first newsletter arrived by post, concealed discreetly in a grey envelope. Wayman opened the envelope and pulled out a glossy, quality print periodical. 'MILE HIGH CLUB WELCOMES BESTSELLING AUTHOR' proclaimed the headline, accompanied by a photo of him and Gwendolyn banging away in the washroom. There was also a welcome letter from the Club President saying how 'excited the Mile High Club was to have Wayman aboard', a membership card, a discount coupon booklet for various restaurants in the Greater London area, a catalogue of Mile High Club merchandise, and a glow-in-the-dark keyring. Wayman hid the contents of the envelope in the back of a closet and poured himself a drink.

The newsletters kept coming, once or twice a week. Wayman had to practically pounce on the postman to get the mail the moment it arrived, lest Margaret see the envelope and get curious. He knew it was only a matter of time before she'd find out. They had been getting along pretty well recently. His new-found success was a spool that handily took up whatever slack was gathering between them. But she was still resentful of his book, which was now hot shit on the bestsellers lists. She kept bringing up references in it that he couldn't even remember writing. She called him a closet misogynist whose understanding of women fell somewhere between Tom Clancy and a street pimp. He didn't bother to defend himself. The critical emasculation and abuse – he supposed he deserved it. That's the price you pay, he figured. At least they were having sex again.

One day a dues notice for fifty pounds arrived with one of the newsletters. They actually wanted *money* from him. Wayman locked himself in his study and rang the number on the newsletter's masthead. A male Scots voice answered, no doubt from a routing centre.

'Mile High Club. How can we help you today?' said the voice effusively.

'Uh . . . I was recently inducted into your club . . .'

'Yes, Mr Barksdale. Welcome.'

Jesus, thought Wayman. They were good. 'Well, I don't really *want* to be a member.'

'I don't understand.'

'I didn't know my ass was going to be plastered across the front page of a publication.'

'I thought you looked quite fetching, sir.'

'Thanks. But if it's all the same to you . . .'

'Mr Barksdale, if it's a question of your outstanding balance, we can work something out whereby . . .'

'I DON'T WANT TO BE IN THE MILE HIGH CLUB!! UNDERSTAND?' Wayman screamed.

There was a pause. 'Well then, Mr Barksdale,' said the voice curtly. 'You're going to have to locate your sponsor . . .'

'My sponsor?'

'. . . and have her or him "unsponsor" you. That's the standard op.'

The voice hung up on him.

Wayman had to go to Heathrow and hang around the SkyLounge, chatting up various flight attendants in order to find out if any of them knew Gwendolyn. He felt like a pervert. Or a terrorist. After about six hours, he was able to ply an address out of a soused BA Flight Deck Officer who'd overheard his enquiries. Apparently, she lived in Chicago.

'Fit bird . . .' he said, wistfully. 'I'll be with you there in spirit!'

Wayman thanked him and headed for the International ticket office.

He flew back to Chicago.

Gwendolyn shared a layover pad, called FlightPath Garden Apartments, with four other attendants, close to Chicago O'Hare. He knocked on the door. She didn't seem all that surprised to see him.

'Hi. How was your flight?' she said, letting him in. Con-airs lay everywhere, like six-shooters. She introduced him to two of her roommates, who did a good job of concealing their disinterest then burrowed into their bedrooms. She offered him a drink and some snacks, which he politely declined. They sat in the living room, amidst a minefield of discarded garments.

Gwendolyn was as chirpy as ever.

'Guy in first class gave me a stock tip today,' she said, somewhat blithely. 'Internet Publishing. You comfy?' She was wearing a pair of right-at-home cowboy boots cut short, which set off her tanned calves nicely. Wayman stole a glance and she caught him.

'Say, how did you find me anyway?'

'Um . . . listen, Gwendolyn . . .'

'Gwen.'

'About this Mile High Club business . . .'

'It's good, isn't it?'

'Well, I . . . uh . . . I don't . . . that was just a fling.

138

The thing in the washroom.'

She cocked her head. 'A *fling?* Is that what it was to you?'

'Well what was it to you?'

'Recruitment.' She seemed insulted. 'A *fling?* What do I look like to you, a tramp?'

Wayman squirmed. 'It's just that I've got a girlfriend at home and I'm trying to make a go of it with her . . .'

She arched an eyebrow.

'. . . and I keep getting these newsletters . . .'

'Well good.'

'No! Not good!! I don't want newsletters. I don't want coupon booklets . . .' his voice was escalating. 'I don't wanna have anything to do with the Mile High Club!'

'Shhhhhh . . . keep your voice down.' She grabbed his arm tightly. 'We're dirty in here,' she whispered.

'What?'

'My roommates could be listening in. Come out on the balcony.'

Under the ear-splitting charge of accelerating jets, Gwendolyn wrote out an address for him.

'I shouldn't be doing this. But you want to talk to Big Patsy.'

'Who's Big Patsy?'

'She's in Houston. Here. It's near the city airport.'

'I'm not flying to Houston. They told me you could get me out of this, Gwendolyn.'

'Listen, if it was my shout, I would. But you're going to have to see Patsy personally on this one.' She gave him a spry kiss on the cheek. 'Good luck.'

Wayman headed back to the airport.

The plane landed at Houston's Hobby Airport (a name that signified no one was taking passenger safety very seriously). He called Margaret and told her he had to make a promotional appearance on a show called *Texas Panorama*. He was frightened by the sheer detail and minutiae of his lies now.

'That's nice for you,' she said sarcastically.

'You could be more encouraging,' he said.

'I'm encouraging you right now. To get home.'

'I meant artistically. What's wrong with you?'

'I'm drowning in my own complacency.'

'You know, Margaret, I could talk to my agent. I'm sure he'd be happy to look at your manuscript.'

'That would make you so happy, wouldn't it. That's it.'

'What's "it"?' he said.

'Little dependencies.'

'I don't see why that has to be an issue, Margaret. We live together. You're entitled to anything.'

'I don't need anything.'

'I'll be home soon,' he said.

'Have a good time in Texas.'

She hung up.

He rented another car and made a quick glide through a mile or so of Houston's finest aerospace real estate. The whole town looked unfinished. Roads changed names for no reason whatsoever and looped back on themselves. He had a hard time believing this was the town that sent folks to the moon. He got on a deserted toll road, which seemed to lose confidence in itself every mile until, suddenly, it just ended. There at the dead end, under a huge billboard that read 'BACK PAIN?' and showed a hazy blown-up photo of a guy looking a little too eager to mangle someone's vertebrae, was the address Gwendolyn had given him. It was a flimsy, one-storey building, totally nondescript. Clearly the only way it had survived was by renting out its roof space for back pain advertising.

Wayman entered the shabby office. It had all the ambience of a betting shop.

'Is this the Mile High Club?' he asked a glum receptionist. Behind her, glummer-looking cubicle types and chattering computers spread out in a random sprawl.

'Yep,' she answered.

'Can I speak with Big Patsy?'

She thumbed toward the rear of the room.

'Check the office.'

Big Patsy wasn't all that big. Dowdy and slightly beleaguered-looking, she half-rose from her desk, stubbed out a cigarette, and motioned for Wayman to sit down.

'Wayman Barksdale,' she rasped. 'Well ain't this a real kick in the pants.' She wore a woolly muffler around her neck as if she might be fighting off a cold or a bout with flu. 'We don't get many famous authors in here. Want a coffee . . .? Dr Pepper?'

'No thanks,' said Wayman, looking around. Blurry snapshots of fornicating frequent fliers covered the walls. The place could have been Larry Flynt's basement. This was all doing his head in. 'Look, I don't know what's going on here. I don't know if this is some sordid blackmail scheme or what, but if you think you can ruin my life—'

'Blackmail scheme?' spluttered Big Patsy. 'What kind of blackmailing scheme offers glow-in-the-dark key rings? We're a club, Mr Barksdale. Have you seen the gift catalogue? There's some real bargains in there. Clock radios, stereos, travel lamps. It's all way below wholesale . . .' She let out a low dieselly snort from the bottom of her throat, winced painfully, then continued. Wayman realised there was something wrong with her larynx. '. . . As for "sordid", well, no one coerced you into having relations with one of our sponsors, did they? It was completely consensual, no?'

Wayman stared at her, flummoxed.

'Well, wasn't it?'

'Yeah. It was consensual.'

'And you enjoyed it?'

'Sort of. I guess.'

'Well then, Wayman. Business is business. Now why don't you own up and pay your dues.'

'No.'

'Or I can just kick up a little dust in the tabloids with that photograph of you and Gwen.'

Wayman paid with a credit card. Big Patsy thanked him then, almost as an afterthought, reached into her desk and pulled out a copy of *The Whore Whisperer*.

'While I gotcha here, how 'bout an autograph? It *was* truly inspirational.'

'I'm glad,' he said. Forlornly, he scribbled 'To Big Patsy' on the frontleaf. 'Not to get too personal,' he said, handing it back to her, 'but how much does a new larynx go for these days?'

He flew home. The ephemerality of fortune, thought Wayman.

It was time to come clean.

Back in London, he waited until the next grey envelope arrived. The morning it did, he carried it, tentatively, into the bedroom where Margaret was seated at a desk, writing. Wayman sat down in a chair across the room,

142

turning the envelope over in his hands. It felt like a death certificate. This wasn't going to be easy.

'What is it?' said Margaret, not looking up from her writing.

'I need to talk to you about something,' he said, stiffly.

She turned in her seat and waited. He stared down at the envelope. How to say this, he thought. That's when he noticed the envelope was actually addressed to *her*.

'What's on your mind?' she said.

new american west
(selected writings)

I'm not from here
But people tell me
It's not like it used to be
They say I should've been here
Back about ten years
Before it got ruined by folks like me
James McMurtry, 'I'm not from here'

Las Vegas

Trapped here for a week doing stand-up comedy for a bunch of fish-faced fossils who would just as soon be downstairs blowing nickels at the slot machines. Most of my material goes through them like a desert breeze. Several people in the crowd appear to be sleeping. I make a crack about Winnebagos, which are those giant metal deathtrap Recreational Vehicles that suck up six or eight lanes of superhighway, bloatmobiles piloted by infirm people who can't see above the dashboard. Every time they fill up on petrol, a new country forms in the Middle-East. Apparently, there must be some Winnebago owners in the audience, because a half-dozen people get up and walk out of the showroom.

I don't know why I come here. To walk the teeming pavements of this town is to battle a tide of slack-jawed human rodentia: a never-ending parade of grifters, drifters, alcoholics, hookers, scam artists, prairie-scum and California detritus, clutching their plastic cups of slot nickels, staring in bovine awe at the monuments of stucco and neon built for their Neanderthal amusement. Men in backwards-worn baseball caps, belt-buckles the size of bin-lids, half-buried beneath cascading beer guts. Jiggly-arsed women with permanently toasted tumbleweeds of hair, frizzed-out, teased up, bedecked in gold rope, their protoplasmic corpulent manatee-shaped bodies sheathed in lamé shell suits. They pour into Caesar's and the MGM Grand, reeling from the fluorescent wash of the pavement, googly-eyed, hoping for a glimpse of Wayne Newton or maybe those annoyingly fey circus twits, Siegfried and Roy.

They queue up and down the Strip for hours, waiting to stuff their gullets at some rancid All-You-Can-Eat Buffet featuring the Unlimited Salad Bar. (Why do they call it a 'bar'? You never see anybody passed out face first in the chickpeas at three in the morning.) Afterwards, bloated and belching toothpicks from their frying pan-shaped faces, they shuffle into showrooms to hear Garth Brooks bend his adenoids or watch a bunch of third-rate hoofers dance like chickens on a hotplate to Michael Flatley's *Lord of the Dance*. (It is doubtful, by the way,

146

that Flatley has ever seen this wayward renegade version of his show.)

The Las Vegas Convention Bureau likes to remind visitors that Las Vegas is now a 'family destination'. Yet there are hookers and porn newsboxes on every corner and the pavement is littered with discarded come-on photos and phone numbers of silicone technologists with names like Tawny and Tiffany, who claim they can 'be in your room in fifteen minutes'. Everywhere you look there are *tits staring up at you from the pavement*, so I suppose Vegas is a real treat for the kids, since an eight-year-old has a closer view of the scenery.

Grown men, seemingly responsible breadwinners, can be found frittering away Junior's university tuition at the Blackjack table, bellowing at no one in particular, 'I don't know how these damned casinos make any money. Hell, they're practically *giving* the rooms away! . . . double down there, mister dealer . . . the drinks are free, for cry-inoutloud . . . double down again . . . and the buffet is what, $3.99 . . . hit me . . . jeez, how does this joint stay in business? Gimme insurance.'

Las Vegas is what America deserves. It is the fastest growing city in the world and the last visible man-made thing an astronaut sees speeding away from the planet. Two thousand years of civilisation and the planet's most visible creation is a lit-up string of clip joints in the Mojave Desert.

The Forum Shops at Caesar's Palace claim to be 'a faithful recreation of ancient Rome'. Presumably, this includes the People Mover (a cornerstone of Roman Civilisation). The People Mover's purpose is – as I understand it – to move people along faster from Point A to Point B. So what do Americans do when they hit the People Mover? *Stop walking entirely*. Everyone bunches

147

up in a frozen rhumba line, trundling along like rotary sushi at roughly $\frac{1}{36}$ of a mile per hour. Amazingly no one seems the least bothered, perfectly content as they are to creep along like God's unclaimed luggage. It's a perfect American device – one which allows you to do nothing at all.

Las Vegas was built for one purpose: to placate people whilst relieving them of their money. It appeals to that substantial percentile of Americans (though not *only* Americans) who are too stupid, complacent and docile to do anything other than eat, gamble, copulate, then eat some more. They are the kind of people who consider themselves to be decent, well-meaning folks, likely to sum up their lives with 'Well, I may just be some good ol' boy from Oklahoma, but by God, I've worked hard and raised a family and taken care of the ones I love!' Well, guess what – *that's what you're supposed to do.* That's minimum requirement for being on the planet! Even a burrow owl knows how to care for its young. Las Vegas rewards the marginal achiever. And it is exactly these kind of complacent, uncomplicated, decent folks who make up Garth Brooks' audience.

I probably don't need to explain who Garth Brooks is but, just for the record, he's a four-foot-one hick. In country music terms he's what's called a Hat Act. He wears a massive cowboy hat and a studded black and white shirt, which resembles Regency linoleum tiles glued to his chubby, weeble-like torso. He sings synthetic, molasses-laden, diabetes-inducing country schmaltz tunes about 'a Bull no one could ride' and having friends in 'low places'. He claims to be faithful to his wife (turns out he isn't) and habitually photo-ops himself with sick kids whilst rendering corn-pone axioms like 'a man never stands so tall as when he stoops to help a child'. I got news for you, Garth. You're forty-nine inches high. You'll never stand tall, full stop.

Live, Garth likes to use a headset microphone, which makes him appear as though he is trying to direct air traffic with a guitar. In his most genuine 'aw shucks, I'm just a country boy done good for hisself' demeanour, he'll humbly thank the quarter of a million people in attendance for making the evening 'special' and 'intimate', and indeed it is, if your idea of 'intimate' is paying to stand amongst a festering throng of clodhoppers watching a plumpy man on an Imax screen.

What Garth has done for country music is to take the vestigial meat and gristle of an authentic American musical form and ladled on to it a cheese-whiz coating Kenny Rogers first perfected in his own country kitchen twenty-five years ago. (Ol' Kenny pretty much took his honey-fried goo-goo musical recipe as far as he could, musically, then opened up a chain of Kenny Rogers Country Fried Chicken parlours around the US, which ultimately went belly-up. He knew when to hold 'em and knew when to fold 'em.) Kenny's vacuum in the music business opened the door for Garth, and boy, has he mined it for every trailer-park dollar he can get his ropin' little hands on.

Where Garth excels is in his masterful and evincing command of metaphors. For example:

> She had a need to feel the thunder
> To chase the lightning from the skies
> To watch the storm, with all its wonder
> Raging in her lover's eyes

From what I can gather, the woman he's singing about seems to be a meteorologist. Anyone who has 'a need to chase lightning' should be kept at arm's length, as far as

I'm concerned. Those lyrics are from a song called 'That Summer' which, from what I can gather, chronicles Garth's teenage dalliance with an older woman.

> She was a lonely widow woman
> Hell bent to make it on her own
> We were a thousand miles from nowhere
> Wheat fields as far as I could see
> Both needin' something from each other
> Not knowin' what that might be.

I know. A car. A vehicle of some sort to facilitate their escape from the Sea of Wheat.

This scenario makes one question Garth's romantic motives. Did he really fancy her? Or was he just another horny teenager a thousand miles from anywhere, stranded beside some nutty prairie widow with a lightning rod on her head?

Here's a jewel from 'Much too Young (To Feel This Damn Old)': 'This old highway is like a woman sometimes.' What kind of woman is he talking about? Stripes and crosshatches painted on her? Bits of roadkill stuck to her body? One who's been laid across seven states? I've been on lots of roads. Not one remotely reminded me of a woman.

But then what do I know? If someone had told me years ago that spewing arbitrary metaphors like that would make me the World's Richest Country Entertainer, I'd've been cranking 'em out like a sausage grinder. 'This old truck is like a Malaysian woman.' 'This old shovel is like an aunt on my Dad's side of the family.' Hey! I could knock that stuff off in my sleep! What *is* Garth Brooks' appeal? He possesses none of the plaintive evocation of Hank Williams, the broke-down bottlehowl of George Jones, not an ounce of the tainted blood that flows through real country music. Garth saccharinised country music to make it palatable to a generation of 4-Wheel-Drive Shopping Mall Foragers, whose idea of rusticity is pouring Ranch Dressing on their salads. And in doing so, he has made himself one of Las Vegas's biggest draws.

Currently you can drive down Las Vegas Strip and within a two-mile stretch pass reproductions of New York City, Luxor, Paris and Venice. In other words, for the lazy terrorist, looking to consolidate his anti-Western impulses into a one-stop bombing experience, Vegas is the place. It has successfully managed to reduce most of the world's cultural and architectural treasures to a collection of over-sized aquarium decor, thus relieving Americans the burden of actually having to *visit* the *real* wonders. One of the newest casinos to open is Steve Wynn's Bellagio, whose garish entrance sign boasts (confoundingly):

NOW APPEARING: CEZANNE, PICASSO, MATISSE

Mr Wynn claims to have designed his hotel for the 'Upscale Vegas Visitor'. 'Upscale' in Las Vegas means anyone who doesn't stub his Marlboro out in the mashed potatoes at the Salad Canoe. Mr Wynn has generously displayed the masterworks of Cezanne, Picasso, Matisse and others on the walls of his casino. I don't think anyone gives a shit. Mr Wynn could hang *The Last Supper* in his casino. People would think it was the entrance to the Buffet.

Salt Lake City

I spent last week in Salt Lake City. If you were to think of Las Vegas and Salt Lake City as the twin headlights

151

of a great truck chugging into the Dark Night of the Great American West, Salt Lake City would be the one with the dim bulb.

One evening I put on my suit and went into a restaurant called Bic'e, which you might assume would be pronounced with an exotic quasi-Italian accent: 'Be-chay'.

'Welcome to Bice,' said the blond hostess. She was wearing a black evening dress and matching black Nikes. Her flashing name badge announced 'Hi! I'm Shauna!'

'One please,' I said.

'One what?' she replied, quizzically.

'Table for one.'

'Wouldn't you prefer to sit at the counter?' Hi! I'm Shauna! said, making the question clearly a demand.

'Yeah, sure,' I said, eyeing the empty counter. The room was a-chatter with tablefuls of animated diners. I was going to be put on display: Mr Lonesome. Mr No-one-will-eat-with-me. Leper boy.

At the counter I was greeted by a wind-burnished bartender whose ski-tan made him resemble an Aryan Nazi raccoon. His name badge read 'Hi! I'm Troy!' Troy had apparently streamlined his verbal repertoire down to one essential word: 'Awesome'.

'Hi, Troy, how are you?' I said, not meaning it.

'Awesome, dude,' he replied.

'What's the special?'

'Aw, dude. It's awesome. You'll be glad you asked. Mahi-Mahi.'

'"Awesome" in terms of size or "awesome" in terms of taste?'

This threw him. Apparently, to Troy, 'awesome' wasn't a word that should beg clarification.

'Well. It's pretty big. And it's grilled in . . . uh . . . some kind of sauce . . .'

'Awe sauce, perhaps?' I said helpfully.

'Yeah,' he said, relieved not to have to work any harder.

'Fine. I'll have the Mahi-Mahi.'

When the dinner arrived, I ordered a beer. Little did I know I had just entered the labyrinthine realm of Utah Drinking Laws. To order alcohol in Salt Lake City is to incur the brutal weight of the Mormons' attempt to induce abstinence through divine bureaucracy.

'You have to be a member,' said Troy.

'Member of what?'

'The club.'

For a moment I thought he was talking about whatever Aryan Raccoon order of the Supreme Awesome Dudes he belonged to, but then I realised he was invoking The State of Utah's Byzantine alcohol statutes.

'Is this a restaurant or a club?' I asked.

'It's a restaurant if you want to eat. It's a club when you want a drink.'

At this point Hi! I'm Shauna! reappeared with some forms for me to fill out.

'It's a five dollar membership fee,' she announced. 'You can bring up to *five* guests with you at any time,' she added, with the slightest undertone of sarcasm, as if I even knew five people.

'So lemme get this straight. I have to pay five dollars just to order a drink with dinner?'

'Yeah.' They both looked at me like this was the most reasonable explanation in the world.

The Mormon religion was founded by a drifter named Joseph Smith, who claimed an angel, Moroni, inexplicably materialised before him one day in the desert and offered him some Golden Tablets. Carved into the tablets was the Book of Mormon, which on inspection suspiciously resembles the King James version of the Bible (almost to a word). As for the golden tablets, no one seems to have found them, which is odd, since this happened in 1833 and there are drinking tankards on the *Antiques Roadshow* that date back to the 1400s. Personally, I find it odd that the religion eschews alcohol consumption since its very pretext – that of a man being given some golden tablets, for no discernible reason, then promptly losing them – has all the components of a cracking good bar story.

I filled out the membership forms, paid my fiver, and was given a Bic'e membership card, which I preciously inserted into my wallet.

'*Now* can I have a beer?' I said to Raccoon-Boy.

'Sure, dude,' he chirped, seemingly oblivious to the ten-minute paper trail I'd just hiked.

'What kind?' he asked.

'What do you have?'

'Wasatch Nut Honeysuckle Brown Ale. ['Wasatch' is the local mountain range.] Wasatch Pale Dry Wheatridge Golden Ale. Dry Cutthroat Pale Amber Wheat Ale. Honey Amber Sweetwheat Pale Ale. Blond Honey Nut Mountain Cherry Dry Amber Ale. BlondAryanRaccoon SupremeAwesomeSkiDudeMonosyllabicNutcakeDrivel Ale . . .'

Apparently, the Mormon onslaught has splintered Utah's beer-making operations into a handful of hippy-dippy microbreweries who've confused beer with pancake syrup.

'Gimme a Budweiser,' I said to Raccoon-Boy.

'Awesome!' he said and went off in search of a Bud.

Five minutes after Raccoon-Boy had delivered my spartan and Honey-Nutless Budweiser a bell went off somewhere. Raccoon-Boy methodically whisked the beer away.

'What's going on?'

'It's midnight. You have to have a special late-night membership to drink after midnight.'

As if on cue, Hi! I'm Shauna! re-materialised with new application forms. Another five bucks changed hands. I filled out the new forms and was presented with yet another membership card.

'What'll you have?' said Raccoon-Boy.

'I'll have a Budweiser,' I said, at which point Raccoon-Boy reached under the counter and presented me with the *same beer I'd been drinking beforehand.*

'Hey,' I said. 'By any chance am I going to have to purchase an early-morning membership when the sun comes up? 'Cause so far it's cost me ten dollars just to *look* at this beer.'

'Nah, we close in half an hour,' he said.

I finished the Golden Mormon Budweiser and left. I can't imagine how Salt Lake handled all the partygoers at the 2002 Winter Games. The paperwork alone must be backed up for a hundred years.

berdoot and brontë:
dubious exposés

THERE IS NO moral ambiguity to travel writing, for geography is above reproach. To see the world vicariously through another's eyes, particularly the illuminated eye of the travel writer, is an idle splendour. This is the genius of the Paul Therouxs, the V.S. Naipauls of the world. They paint for us that which is already painted, and we are thankful.

Of course any discussion of serious travel writing will doubtlessly include the work of Wink Berdoot. His contributions to *Wings* (the in-flight magazine of Skyways Airlines) would constitute a sizeable and daunting read even to the most intrepid armchair traveller. But Berdoot is not one to confine his talents to a single in-flight publication, no matter how prestigious. His work is just as apt to be found in *Horizons* (the in-flight magazine of Rocky Mountain Airways), *Gateways* (MidBritish Airways) or

Nomad (Costa Rican Airlines), as well as countless other high-altitude publications. You can't rope the wind, I suppose. Whether he is describing, in vibrant detail, a good Tex-Mex restaurant in San Antonio, or vividly heralding the new trend in fat-tyre BMX bikes, or just sardonically ruminating on 'those infernal automated voice-option menus', Berdoot is a literary voice to be reckoned with. And, unlike Theroux, Naipaul, Chatwin or Mayles, whose ability to hold the reader through sheer writing talent might be considered by some to be a bit of a one-trick pony, Berdoot quite often supplements his articles with a photograph or two.

Such is the calibre of his writing, I have often found myself booking an airline flight on the offchance I might find one of his articles in the in-flight publication. One thing is certain – the scenery out of the window is secondary when Wink Berdoot is on board. He is doubtlessly the most charismatic and compelling of the new breed of In-flight Magazine Writers.

Lately, however, some have questioned the legitimacy of Berdoot's work. In fact, in less reverential circles, the word 'plagiarism' has been bandied about. While Berdoot himself has defended his writing, stating defiantly that his integrity has never wavered, some blatant similarities to the work of other in-flight writers have surfaced recently. Consider the following passage from a Berdoot article that appeared in the April issue of *ALOHA* (the in-flight magazine of All Hawaii Airlines):

Maui, Hawaii: QUINCY'S, Wailea Resort
(808–555–6754). Perfect late-night cuisine. Sinfully delicious and reasonably priced. Enjoy gorgeous views from the terrace overlooking the ocean.

Without question, an evocative piece of writing. But it is uncomfortably close to an article written by a certain Jan Purcevelt for *Avia* (the in-flight magazine of AirCal Airlines) almost six months earlier:

> RICO'S, 16 South Bay (760) 555–5678 (Reservations), is the perfect late-night spot. It is reasonably priced and the desserts are sinfully delicious. Enjoy splendid views from the terrace overlooking the ocean.

Now, no one's reputation is being called into question here. It's quite possible this is an example of one writer 'absorbing' the style of another. Powerful writing can have that effect on someone. Besides, there are a lot of terraces and a lot of oceans out there, so maybe we're just talking coincidence. Unfortunately, this is not an isolated example. Consider the following excerpt from *Pathways* (the in-flight magazine of Canada Airlines):

> . . . with 18 holes of golf, 10 tennis courts, a four-star gourmet restaurant *and* a gigantic conference centre, The VANDERBILT is a world unto itself. Recently restored to its original splendour, the rooms offer spectacular views and, best of all, big fluffy towels you can almost get lost in.

The scope and grandeur of this writing is quintessentially Berdootesque, right down to the trademark technique of describing hotel linen. Indeed, Berdoot *did* pen the article. But if one were to peruse the *Spotlight on Scotland* section of Aer Caledonie's *Tartan Flier*, one would come across the following text:

> McCLELLAN'S BEN NEVIS RESORT: If an 18-hole

159

course, 10 tennis courts and a gigantic conference centre is your idea of a world unto itself, this is the place for you. Recently restored to its original Edwardian splendour, the rooms are nice and spacious and feature large fluffy towels.

Again, the *Tartan Flier* article was published almost three years ago. But let's not jump to conclusions. Even if numerous other examples have come to light:

. . . this handy little gadget promises to propel tele-conferencing into the 21st century
('Tech Talk' by Wink Berdoot, *Horizons Magazine*, June 2001)

. . . this handy gadget is the first great teleconfer-encing device of the 21st century
('What's New in the Office', *EnFlight Magazine*, May 2001)

or consider:

Cairo is another world . . .
('Mysterious Cairo' by Wink Berdoot, Skystreams, April 2000)

Tunis is another world . . .
('Unravelling the Mysteries of Tunis' by Eunice VanDer Smyck, Takeoff, July 1999)

Mr Berdoot has defended his overall methods. 'I don't just trot out facts and descriptions,' he is quoted as saying. 'I try to tell the reader a story. I try to take the reader someplace. I've *been to these places*! I've *seen* these gadgets. So, to accuse me of stealing someone's writing is to accuse me of stealing their experiences, their lives. Do I look like someone who would steal a life? Are you calling me a murderer, you little piss-ant?'

Berdoot initially defied his critics to find other 'borrowed' sentences and passages. When confronted with readily available examples he was angry to the point of being apoplectic. 'I challenge you to find another writer who weaves such brilliant narrative and detailed observation into a seamless whole, one of the best travel books of the last decade,' he said, somewhat cryptically. 'Plus I'm insightful, as well as helpful. An invaluable travel accessory! Runs on 110 or 220.' For no discernible reason, he added, 'Rio de Janeiro *sizzles*!'

Confounding though that explanation may be, Berdoot's work continues to be both economic and prolific. He is currently hard at work on an article for *Horizons* (Rocky Mountain Airways) on 'the funny side of cats'. 'You know,' he says, 'like when they see something that isn't really there. Which causes *you* to freak out.'

Obviously, Wink Berdoot isn't afraid to show his lighter side. Me, I'm booking a flight and planning to delve into some high-calibre reading.

* * *

The literary world was set on its ear recently with the announcement that a new work by Charlotte Brontë had come to light. The alleged tome, about Luddites and woolworkers in Yorkshire, presented by an antiquarian bookseller from Edinburgh, bears an unarguable stylistic similarity to Ms Brontë's previous works. Still, we should hedge our bets on its authenticity. We don't need another embarrassing cultural hoax like the one perpetrated last year by a pair of British archaeologists, who claimed to have discovered two more Sheen–Estevezes and a new Baldwin brother under a giant slab of granite in southern France (which turned out to be a big PR prank).

The book dealer, one Mr Ian King, reputedly fed lengthy sections of the book into his computer to establish some kind of literary DNA link with Ms Brontë's earlier writings – in particular *Jane Eyre*, *Shirley* and her seldom read but highly amusing chick-lit account of a holiday excursion on the Indian ocean called *Hey! There's a hissing Madagascar cockroach in my bra!!* Among the catchwords and phrases Mr King's modem spat out were 'terribleness', 'horribles' and 'Old Mr Cranky Pants', all vintage Brontëisms. Also, several ancillary characters from *Jane Eyre* reappear, much more fleshed out in the 'new' book, which, depending on the source you choose to consult, is entitled either *Sarah Miles* or *Charlotte Brontë's How to Have Buns of Steel in 30 Days*.

One such character is August Finny, described in *Jane Eyre* as 'a languid man who seemed composed of a swarthy guile'. In *Sarah Miles*, Ms Brontë takes him a step further by describing him as having the erotic appeal of 'a young Andy Garcia. 100% hot!! He sauntered into the room and ladies went moist.' Unfortunately this passage raises as many questions as it answers. The reference to Andy Garcia in a book purported to be written in 1845 is certainly a red flag for anyone just itching to yell 'HOAX!!' Still, there's never been any question that Ms Brontë was a visionary, so I, for one, am willing to let it go.

What troubles me more is a passage roughly halfway through the 'manuscript'. (I use the term 'manuscript' loosely. The entire story was scrawled – for reasons unknown – on the back of 419 shovels in *very* tiny lettering, and uncovered in a tool shed by a Yorkshire gardener

162

named Thad Cruddles, who first dismissed it as 'mindless doodling'. Cruddles noticed the words 'Property of Charlotte B' inscribed at the bottom of each shovel – a distinctive trademark of Ms Brontë, who shared a flat with her two sisters, Emily and Moosey, and instinctively marked all her personal possessions.) The passage seems stylistically out of character for Ms Brontë's murky prose:

> The night was dark and quivering and there was scarce enough light to make the street visible. Dora felt a terribleness within as she passed the stone church. She pulled her shawl tight to her wan, flaxen face. Then, she turned the corner and heard the first few rifts of some hot be-bop wafting out of a neon-lit little dive called Smoky Joe's. Dora stepped inside and hipped herself to the wicked woolly vibes a Luddite cat was layin' down on the skins . . .

It strikes me as idiosyncratic that Luddite woolgatherers would be listening to bebop, but then, I'm no expert on jazz. I've always found it a bit abstruse.

The more cogent question, for me, anyway, is *why* was *Sarah Miles* never published? Without question it is an important literary work and at the time of its completion, Ms Brontë was a very popular author, so you'd think *someone* would have put the book up for sale, if for no other reason than one can always use a good shovel. I posed this question to Sandra Chalford, director of the Brontë Museum in Haworth. (Ms Chalford is also the creator of the hit one-woman show *Charlotte Brontë: Comin' at Ya!!*) Ms Chalford informed me that the book had indeed been published, but under a different name. Apparently, Ms Brontë had wanted to put her own name on the book but at the time there was a worldwide shortage of umlauts and Charlotte, perfectionist that she was, wouldn't settle for 'Bronte' without the two little dots. Thus the book was attributed to Charles Bukowski.

Doubtless, there are those who will presume Mr King to be a huckster, but really, what possible fortune or notoriety could he derive from claiming to have found a new book by Charlotte Brontë? Hollywood isn't exactly licking its lips for the screen rights. The book is about Luddites and wool, for chrissake. Unless it features a talking sheep as a central character, I don't see HIT written on it.

pie chart man

Y OU MAY NOT be aware of this but I am, in addition to being a thoroughly entertaining comedian, one of the world's foremost Pie Chart Men. Let me explain. Every major newspaper is required to keep on staff a trained statistician who can – at a moment's notice – transform dull facts and figures into colourful and entertaining pie charts. That's your Pie Chart Man. It is a unique talent, one that requires the combined skills of a Geometrist, Statistical Analyst, Graphic Illustrator and Piemaker.

Few are qualified for this precise and daunting science. I guess I've been blessed.

Not to blow my own horn, but I'm a goddamned good Pie Chart Man. I started with the *Baltimore Sun* way back in '76. I was only seventeen years old at the time, having graduated from Harvard with a Masters in Advanced Mathematics. At the time I was in the Cartoon Colour Corrections Department, but when the *Sun's* Pie Chart Man – a trusty and well-liked fella named Inky Somers –

died in a bundlebin accident, they moved me right into his slot. I picked up the game pretty quickly.

You never knew what the *Sun* was gonna throw at you.

'Richie, big fella,' my first editor, Gene 'Hap' Howard, would bark, popping his blistery red pate over my cramped cubicle, the one I shared with a crosswords editor. 'Seems Baltimorians are buying washer/dryer combos in record numbers!! It's damned exciting! Whip me up a pie chart on front-loaders vs top-loaders, will you? And have it on my desk by five p.m.!!'

That's the kind of pressure cooker I had to operate in. We didn't have laptops in those days. Internets, hah! You scratched and bled for every morsel of info you could scavenge.

In this particular example: first you get on the horn to the big three appliance giants: Westinghouse, Amana, Hotpoint . . . to get some solid sales figures. You run makes and models, find out who's paying cash, who's on the layaway plan. In other words: stats, stats, stats (in the business we call this 'laying the crust'). Then you cross-reference the sales figures with a geographical breakdown of standard statistical metropolitan areas, factored into median household density. Then you amortise that figure across the entire socio/economic strata. Sorry to use so many fifty cent words, but there's no layman's way to explain it.

Next, of course, the planar format has to be converted into a basic geometric circle using Euclidean Calculus. Then you illustrate the whole thing with some stickman figures. Believe me, it takes a special talent.

I worked for all the big papers: the *San Francisco Chronicle*, the *Wall Street Journal*, *Le Figaro* (my official title was *homme de la graphique du quiche*). And *USA Today*, the bible of pie charts.

Nowadays, I just do freelance work, speciality gigs.

Papers from all over the world ring me when they're in a Pie Chart quandary. Of course nowadays, with diminishing attention spans, the old-fashioned sectional Pie Chart is rapidly giving way to more dramatic, eye-catching forms of creative abstracting (or as I call them – pieless Pie Charts). Just last week, for example, I got a call from Bill Gates. Rather, I should say, Bill Gates' publicist, Chesty LePate. Chesty and I go back a few years.

'Richie,' said Chesty. 'Bill and I were sitting around the micro-lounge the other day, just kinda shootin' the breeze, when Bill started up on how much money he has. You know that's one of Bill's favourite topics . . . anyhow, he comes up with a real corker. "Chesty? If I were to pile all my money under my mattress, then fell out of bed . . . how long you reckon it would take me to hit the ground?"'

I knew what Chesty was about to throw at me, and already my analytical oven was preheating.

'We talking one-dollar bills?' I asked Chesty.

'Yepper.'

'I'll have the answer by Monday morning,' I said, and went right to work.

Not a difficult problem but a time-consuming one. The basic formula is pretty cut and dried:

$$\frac{\text{fiscal units x density of currency}}{\text{altitude}} \times \text{terminal velocity of plummeting Bill Gates} = ?$$

The answer, as I'm sure you've deduced, *would appear* to be eighteen minutes. But that's where you would be wrong, which is why *I'm* a Pie Chart Man and you're some schmo on the street. Because what you failed to take into account is, even as Bill Gates is falling, his money is earning interest – which has be factored into the descent. Thus, if you shovelled the *interest* on Bill Gates' money under the mattress *as he was falling*, technically, Bill Gates would actually never hit the ground. The man is richer than gravity.

Another way of looking at it is: Bill Gates is so loaded, he's immortal. Thus the phrase 'you can't take it with you' doesn't apply to Bill Gates. He's not going anywhere. He's suspended in mid-air by his own wealth.

I whipped together a vibrant, colourful Pie Chart, which actually featured a stickman caricature of Bill (wearing his prescription ashtray glasses on his head, which also factored into his descent), and faxed it over to Chesty.

He called me the following day to inform me Mr Gates was personally upset with the inconclusive status of his falling-out-of-bed scenario.

'Bill needs something a little more concrete,' said Chesty. 'He doesn't like the idea of being functionally suspended in mid-air.'

Jesus, what an ego, I thought to myself.

So I took a more geophysical tack and put Bill's money into a Global Economic Pie. I thought it might chuff him to know how many countries he was richer than. The answer I arrived at is slightly astounding. (But true!) *Bill Gates is wealthier than all but eighteen countries on the planet*. Thus, technically Bill Gates is the nineteenth richest country in the world. He should change his name to Bilgaria.

You would think this kind of incontrovertible Pie Chart Evidence would at least warrant a thank-you call from that bespectacled prick. But no. Oh well, I never said it wasn't a thankless job.

voices

EVERYONE, AT SOME point, hears voices in their heads. That doesn't necessarily mean you should listen to them. Often people who pay too much attention to voices end up in prison, in administrative segregation, which of course makes things worse because there *no one* talks to you and the voices in your head are your only friends and say things to you like 'make a spear out of dining-room cutlery and take an art teacher hostage', which is what Charles Bronson did not too long ago . . .

Bronson (not the actor), is a former bare-knuckle fighter, circus strongman and currently reigning 'world record holder for tossing dwarves' (according to a BBC news report), who also happens to be one of Britain's most notorious prisoners. Obviously the first question that comes to most people's minds is, 'Where did Charles Bronson go wrong?' (My first thought, however, is 'Exactly what category of dwarf-tossing are we talking about; distance or numbers of dwarves tossed?') Anyway,

Bronson got a little peeved at his art teacher for making some disparaging comments about Bronson's drawings. So he held a makeshift spear to the guy's throat, donkey-paraded him around Hull Prison for about forty-two hours, force-fed him some chunks of tinned pineapple and generally made the guy regret he'd ever belittled Bronson's delicate depictions of furry woodland creatures bedecked in tiny pastel swastikas. If you ask me, the teacher had it coming. What do you gain by telling a psychopath his work is pedantic? The important thing is, *the guy isn't hurting anyone while he's doodling with his crayons, is he???* No, he's not. No dwarves are being randomly hurled about. Britain's prison rehab system hums nicely when its inmates are just biding their time, trying to stay within the lines. Why stir things up? Idiot.

Clearly, Bronson is prone to overreaction. A more rational person might have waited for a number of criticisms from a number of different critics before taking any hostages. Then, it's just an artistic backlash. This, I suppose, is what separates psychopaths from normal people. It's important to remember: *the first voice you hear in your head is usually wrong.*

In his trial during the late seventies David Berkowitz, more often known as Son of Sam, claimed that a neighbour's black Labrador urged him to kill and maim thirteen people in the Queen's/Brooklyn area of New York City. Let's assume that's true. Admittedly, anyone who found a dog talking to them might be initially impressed. But if the dog said to you, 'Hey there, mister, do us a favour. Nip out and kill some people,' wouldn't you *at the very least* lean down to the dog and say, 'Baaaaaaad boy. Baaaaaad dog!' Of course you would.

Nowadays, from his cell, Berkowitz maintains that

170

Jesus tells him what to do. And ever since he started listening to Jesus, no one's been hurt. In other words, if you're a psychopath, always try to get a second opinion before acting on commands.

Which brings us, as it would, to Charlie Manson. These days Charles spends most of his time behind bars polishing up his dissertations on earth's need to preserve what he calls 'ATWA' (air, trees, water, animals). He also spends a lot of time at prison Alcoholics Anonymous meetings. Good to see ol' Chucky's given up the booze because, frankly, when your drinking starts to get in the way of your psychopathic behaviour . . . you're in trouble.

You can actually view Manson's artwork (which includes festively coloured scorpions fashioned from string beads) at his web site, and lemme tell you, compared to the childish doodlings of Charles Bronson, the man's got some chops.

Again we're dealing with someone whose excessive behaviour was guided by unseen voices, namely the Beatles. Manson claims it was the lyrics to 'Helter Skelter' that exhorted him and his disciples to carve up seven people in California in the late sixties. This earned him a life sentence as well as the inglorious blame for ruining the Hippie Decade. My question has always been, just *what* part of 'Helter Skelter' was Manson responding to?

> When I get to the bottom I go back to the
>   top of the slide
> Where I stop and I turn and I go for a ride
> Till I get to the bottom and I see you again

I can't quite seem to glean from those lyrics any suggestion of binding people up with gaffer tape and poking them with a fork, which is what Charlie did. But then, I'm not a big fan of the Beatles.

If only Mr Manson had waited a few years for more cogent instructions from one of the Beatles. Here, for example, is a verse from Paul McCartney that I personally find very disturbing:

> Someone's knockin' at the door
> Somebody's ringin' the bell
> Someone's knockin' at the door
> Somebody's ringin' the bell
> Do me a favour
> Open the door
> And let 'em in!!!

The reason I find this disturbing is because McCartney made a shitload of money from that song, whereas I've uttered those same words a number of times in my life and never made a lousy dime off the deal! (Don't even get me started on 'Here Comes the Sun'.)

If only Manson had waited for that later, more logical voice. No one would be dead. At worst, he would have let in a draught.

savage journeys

Actual Film Blurbs

Fear and Loathing in Las Vegas: A savage journey into the heart of the American Dream

Terminus America: A journey into the dark heart of the American Dream

Wilding (starring Joey Travolta): Tommy, a product of the American Dream. But the dream turns into a nightmare

Apocalypse Now: A waking nightmare underlies . . . the failure of the American Dream

Stroscek (Werner Herzog): A journey into the Great American Nightmare

American Beauty: Explores the hollow darkness of the American Dream . . . and nightmare

American Nightmare: 'I wanted something savage to happen' (director John Carpenter, promoting his new

173

feature on the Independent Film Channel)
The Deer Hunter: '(John) Savage embarks on a hunting trip before leaving for the great nightmare . . .' *Film Review*

Maybe it's just me, but over the past twenty years or so a lot of films seem to have been promising travel packages they've not quite been able to live up to. There's nothing more infuriating than plopping down a fistful of cash for the promise of a Nightmare Journey only to have the lights come up two hours later to discover you're merely sitting with your feet in a runny pool of popcorn butter. My advice is to get off your lazy ass and make the journey yourself. Allow me to give you some travel tips.

First of all, as a travel destination, The American Dream isn't all it's cracked up to be. Having made several visits, I can attest to that. The first could have benefitted from better planning. Bear in mind that a Nightmare Journey is a fairly fraught mode of travel – it's not for everyone. Half the fun of any trip is getting there, so if you choose to travel by Nightmare I suggest you find a reputable one. The Nightmare I chose was pretty dodgy. In fact, I kept waking up a lot. Then when I finally got to the American Dream, wouldn't you know it, it didn't even exist. Fucking rip-off, if you ask me.

My second trip was even worse. I opted for the Dark Journey into the Heart of the American Dream. (Stupidly, I'd convinced myself that the American Dream *did* indeed exist, I'd just gone to the wrong place to look for it.) Having eschewed the Nightmare form of transportation, this time I was able to stay awake for the whole thing. But wouldn't you know it, the journey was so dark, I couldn't see a goddamned thing. *Read the small print.* I tried to get my money back, but was informed that the

American Dream is not only nonexistent but also non-refundable.

Do not mistake The Heart of the American Dream for America's Dark Heart. As ethereal clichés go, they may sound similar, but believe me, the difference between the Heart of the American Dream and America's Dark Heart is like the difference between a day at Wet&Wild and a jar of Dizzy Gillespie's trumpet spit, and I don't think I can put it any more succinctly than that. As in the above-mentioned Dark Journey, remember, you won't be able to see the Dark Heart when you arrive at it. So if it's sightseeing you're after, you may want to consider a Savage Journey into Something Lighthearted.

Savage Journey vs Nightmare Journey: here, again, it depends on your level of comfort. The Savage Journey will likely take you through some vicious terrain. Lots of para-noid, psychotic characters, isolated settings and more than a fair share of foreshadowing. The Nightmare Journey is more one of introspection: self-delusion, moral ambiguity, religious symbolism, that sort of stuff. If it comes down to a matter of which is more relaxing, I'd go with Nightmare. You get to sleep in. The Savage Journey will have you up every morning at dawn, answering the door to some creepy dude with misshapen teeth and bluish gums, wielding a handgun due, invariably, to a case of mistaken identity.

One final note: beware offers for Journeys that purport to being 'Twisted' or 'Harrowing', as you'll invariably find these far too obtuse and perplexing to put up with for long. Also, you'll probably end up stranded in the middle of nowhere. As a rule of thumb, Twisted and Harrowing Journeys seldom arrive at the Heart of *anything* American. They usually go to the Soft Underbelly of America. Which is a tourist hellhole.

cutting horses

I LIVE (SOMETIMES) IN Montana. It is big, rugged, cowpoke country – somewhat mythical – inhabited by codgers, coots, misfits, guys in ten-gallon hats and women with the hair to fill them. A good number of them are natives, an equally good number, like me, drifted there. I know my place and I try to defer to the long-timers who have seen the stretch marks Montana has had to endure.

When you move to some place special the tendency is to want to kick the ladder out from beneath you. And when the big money arrives, you know the joint is going to be ruined. Sadly, the Big Money has arrived in Montana. Ted Turner, Steven Seagal, Calvin Klein; all are now Montana Land Barons. Million Dollar Misfits. Goddamn.

Last week there was a tiny ad in my home town newspaper advertising a World-Class Executive Cutting Horse Seminar, to be held in July:

An excellent opportunity for CEOs and top-level business leaders to hone their decision-making skills astride a champion-breed cutting horse

In case you don't know what a cutting horse is, let me explain. It is a horse specially trained to separate ('cut') calves from a herd. It is a nimble and canny skill 'requiring an instinctual symbiosis between horse and rider'. For some reason, executives are supposed to find this activity sharpens their corporate chops. The advertised cost for the seminar was $5,000, exclusive of air fare. You would think maybe the first skill these guys would want to master would be skilfully avoiding paying five grand just to climb on the back of a horse to annoy some calves.

Since when does pinning a calf against a fence correlate to running a corporation? If you ask me, these guys just want to play Hoss Cartwright, trade in their double-breasted pinstripes and swivel chairs for a bronco saddle, transport their massive, thirsty, corporate egos to some theme-park version of another time. What happened to riding the golf range in a cushioned go-kart? Do they *have* to be cowboys, mountaineers, balloonists? How come you never hear about a dry cleaner scaling Mount Everest? Why does Richard Branson feel the need to travel around the world in a balloon? He *owns* an airline. He can travel around the world in sixteen hours. (That's impressive enough for us, Richard. Now shut up and go make us some more diet cola.)

Look, if you're rich, bored and restless, fine, but you don't have to alert the world every time you undertake a recreational pursuit. My uncle is a bank president in a small town in Kentucky. But he doesn't call a press conference every time he drags out his bass boat.

* * *

Anyway, back to the Execu-pokes. Perhaps they don't care how oafish they appear amongst the native and near-native Montanans, but man o' man you can spot then coming down the pike. The boots are always a giveaway. Spiffy Tony Llamas made, quite likely, from an exotic species like ostrich or alligator (though ironically *not* from llamas), dappled in phosphorescent green or purple. You might as well wear a sign on your back saying 'Kick the shit out of me now'. Then there's the hat. It is extremely difficult to wear five pounds of stiffened felt on your head and not look self-conscious about it. Real cowboys look like they were welded into their hats, which have been crushed into submission then lacquered in dust, tobacco juice, cowshit and their favourite brand of tequila. Real cowboys know to duck when they enter a doorway. Cow-execs look like they're trying to balance a fruit and cheese platter on their heads. If accompanied by wives, the wives will invariably be dangling some mudflap-sized sterling silver howling coyotes from their earlobes. (For some inexplicable reason, 'well-heeled' women who visit Montana immediately gravitate to these goofy prairie baubles. The coyote is one of God's most malnourished and scavenging creatures. Why it has been romanticised in women's fashion jewellery is a mystery.)

As a rule, the more weighty stuff on your head, the more out-of-town you are.

So there's your Weekend Wrangler couple, dressed up like dudes and dudettes, tooling around in rented Land Rovers, oblivious to the smirks and derision of the locals. They have to have the most 'elegantly rugged' accom-modation, the best horse, the plumpest saddle. Everything Top Shelf.

But when Mr Cow-exec mounts his cutting horse, he finds, despite the promise of 'symbiosis', he actually has

9–11

THERE ARE DATES in our lives we are destined to
remember always. For me, September 11 2001 is
certainly one of them. Let me tell you, brother, I *learned*
something about mankind that day. And I learned something about myself and what's truly important to me.

The day began mundanely enough. I awoke to a bright
blue sky. There was just a smattering of autumn crisp-
ness in the air. I went out into the backyard to quaff a
coffee and spend some time with Pedro, my dachshund.
Then, at about ten-thirty, my neighbour Trudy Murtaugh
leaned out her window and called over to me. She seemed
distressed.

'I think there's something wrong with your dog,' she
said. 'He's been scratching all morning.'

I lifted Pedro on to my lap and examined him. Sure
enough, he was covered with dry patchy spots.

I drove him to the vet. Seems the morning was turning
out to be not so good. When I got to the vet, the place

was eerily quiet. I waited at the help desk for almost five minutes. Finally an assistant came out and took Pedro from me and examined him.

'Horrible morning,' she said, combing through his fur.

And she was right. Turns out little Pedro had eczema! After I paid the bill, a lousy $200 – *just for some shots and dog eczema medicine* – I went outside and, wouldn't you know it, my car wouldn't start. I put Pedro on a leash and started the long walk home. Jeezus, what a dumper of a morning *this* was turning out to be.

The vet nurse had put one of those little plastic funnel things around Pedro's neck, which meant he had to trot around looking like a lampshade with legs. It was humiliating for the poor little guy and on the way home some winos flicked some cigarette butts right into his lampshade. Drunken, insensitive assholes.

I called the tow company and asked if they could come and rescue my car, which was still parked at the vets.

'Could you call back in a few hours,' someone drawled on the other end of the line, and quickly hung up. A few hours!! What the hell was going on there? I'd heard a TV blaring in the background so it wasn't like they were swamped with work or anything. I sat there and shook my head. This was turning out to be one of the shittiest days of my life.

Believe it or not, *it got worse*. Turns out, when the mechanic finally showed up, I'd blown a head gasket. I called my insurance company to see if I was entitled to a loaner and those bastards didn't even answer the phone. I finally ended up, around five in the afternoon, at one of those Luxury Rental joints out in the valley. They were the only people I could find open! I musta walked about six and a half miles to get there. I had to bring Pedro with me, because the vet had told me to keep an eye on him. Lemme tell you, six miles to a dachshund is like a fucking triathlon. The dog has only got three-inch legs. I had to carry him most of the way. When I arrived, the only guy there – who wasn't even a rental agent but a mechanic, for chrissakes – shambled out on to the lot and started going on and on about 'A-rab terrorists' or something. Frankly I didn't need to hear this shit. When I finally got around to engaging his attention, he told me the only car he had available to rent was a vintage '55 Thunderbird. Can you believe that? What the hell am I going to do with a '55 T-bird?

I didn't have a whole hell of a lot of choice so I forked over another $200 for rental, plus a deposit of $500. So far September 11 2001 had cost me almost a grand and the sun hadn't even gone down!

I lowered myself into the seat of the car, feeling like a goddamned pimp or something. The mechanic, who seemed preoccupied to begin with, wasn't all too sure about me. You could tell he was apprehensive about me even driving the damned car, especially after Pedro jumped in and dumped cigarette butts all over his precious fucking floorboards.

Now for the capper – the incident that will always remind me what a *crappy day* September 11 2001 was for me (and from what I understand, *nobody* had all that great a day on September 11) – as I was rolling out of the car lot, one of those big high-tech remote control security gates trundled out of its recess and, with a sickening crunch, caved in the whole driver's side door. I'm not lying – just crumpled it like a Pepsi can. I couldn't believe it. The metal gate came to a rest about six inches from my rib cage.

'Holy Shit, friend,' I said, crawling out of the passenger's side door. 'You oughta fix your gate!'

'You oughta teach your dog not to sit on the remote control,' he replied. I looked over at Pedro and goddamn if it wasn't true, he was sitting right on the damn thing.

Ended up costing me my deposit.

I heard some people talking on TV, jaw-boning about whether September 11 had changed us, as a country. Some woman, one of them media types, said no, we're just as arrogant and self-centred and oblivious to the plight of others as ever. Well, I thought about firing off a letter to that gal to tell her she was *absolutely right*. We're still the same bunch of insensitive assholes we always were. I can't believe that sonofabitch car rental guy kept my deposit. How the fuck is a dachshund supposed to know it's sitting on a remote control?

I learned on September 11, the hard way, that if your car breaks down and you have to rent one, be careful who you rent from, cause a lot of those places are ripoff joints. Get used to taking the bus, friend.

gumball minutes

*L*AST WEEK THE *Ford Penny Gumball Company held its annual stockholders meeting. Penny gumball machines are still fairly prevalent throughout America. They usually sit at the entrance to variety stores. They dispense gumballs. For a penny.*

The stockholders and executives usually stay at the El Cortez. The big meeting, which takes place in the Conquistador Room, is the pivotal part of the trip. Following are the minutes from this year's Annual Report.

11:00 a.m.: Annual meeting of the Ford Gumball Stockholders convenes with a call-to-order by President Chubb Ford III, who welcomes the stockholders and unveils the sales theme for 2003: 'Ford Gumballs: King of the Chews'. He displays a toastmaster's expertise for humour by recounting an incident from the previous evening. Seems Mrs Ford, in a frenzy of adoration, accidentally threw the keys to their Cadillac Coupe De Ville at Tom Jones while he was performing onstage at the MGM Grand. She'd *meant* to throw her room key at him. They had to engage a security guard to retrieve the car keys from Mr Jones, who was actually attempting to speed away from the casino carpark in the couple's automobile when the guard intercepted him. 'It's not unusual!' Ford III cackled, though the subtlety of this remark was lost on most of the attendees. Or maybe they'd heard that overripe little *bon mot* too many times already.

11:09 a.m.: Deputy Comptroller Woodward 'Woody' Sigurdson delivers the first bit of bad news for the morning, announcing that profits are down for the thirty-seventh consecutive year. Average weekly gumball output per dispenser was now 18.3. Doing some quick figuring, most stockholders were able to deduce this came out to 18.3 cents per week per gumball machine. However, taking into account the 'slug factor' (phony metal tokens or Guatemalan pesos, both the same size as American pennies) the Gumball Unit Average (GUA) was actually closer to 16.5 per week. At this point, several stockholders, perhaps in a mild panic, strongly questioned why Ford III still used armoured trucks to make the weekly collections from the machines. Someone wondered aloud why they 'just didn't get some homeless guy or "Retired Service Geezer" to go around every once in a while and empty the damned things'. His suggestion was duly noted by Mr Ford III.

11:21 a.m.: Comptroller Sigurdson breaks down the expenditures for the year 2002:

PRODUCTION COSTS	$118,967.43
SALARY & WAGES	$115,411.96
DISPENSER MAINTENANCE	
(removing hardened wads of gum plugged into coin slots by disenchanted purchasers and listless kids)	$3,941.00
DESIGN, RESEARCH & DEVELOPMENT	$18,491.50
	$256,811.89

This figure, weighed against a net annual profit of $816.33, came to an annual net loss of $255,995.56. Everyone took a few moments to let the gravity of this number settle in. Then, President Ford III, with his usual brusque optimism, asserted that 'things were looking up for '03!'.

'People will be looking for something to spend their penny on in the coming year!' he waxed. 'This business is cyclical. You roll with the punches.' His optimism was so stalwart as to border on cretinism.

Someone pointed out that more people were flinging loose pennies down the sewer gratings than spending them on gumballs. Mr Ford III expressed dismay at this. He was equally resentful of the Comptrollers suggestion that the only way to turn a profit in the coming year was to 'jack up the price of a gumball to $6,500 apiece.'

'What kind of person would pay $6,500 for a gumball?' Ford III shouted, his optimism now visibly waning. He quickly dismissed the idea, citing that such a price increase would elevate the gumball out of the 'impulse item' category into something more akin to a 'Fabergé egg'. It was an interesting analogy and Comptroller Sigurdsen responded by calling Ford III an 'Amazing

Shithead', then resigning. The assistant Comptroller, Doug Hawthorne, pushed the idea further, by presenting a projected-cost analysis of the '65-G' prototype gumball. He had also worked up several options for financing gumballs, through either one's local bank or a finance company. He stressed that the company needed to sell only about thirty-five a year at $6,500 to turn a profit.

11:29 a.m.: A general debate followed, discussing the pros/cons of retooling dispensers to accept $6,500 in pennies. But Ford III refused to authorise the price increase. 'Penny Gumballs have a place in America's heart,' he said. 'Some things aren't about profit. They're about the joy on a kid's face when he holds a colourful orb of chicle in his tiny palm.' It was a passionate and heartfelt statement, and it reminded everyone of why they went into this business in the first place.

11:41 a.m.: The entire discussion is tabled because Research & Development are anxious to bring out the new line of colours for 2003. They include green, red, blue, yellow and white. Everyone applauds and the meeting seems to end on a high note. For another year, at least, the penny gumball seems assured of survival.

the thithterton

FEW THEATRES HAVE had more impact on me than Auckland's now relegated-to-dust Thithterton. To call it the Grand Old Dame of New Zealand's theatres would be a misrepresentation, for it wasn't particularly grand or old and it certainly wasn't a dame, but more like a voluptuous Italian peasant daughter dressed in black with olive juice glistening about her ankles while in the distance a boatman sings lustily – that's what the Thithterton was to me. It was a precious jewel of Auckland's harbour, a beckoning lump of concrete, so rare and precious in its absolute nondescription, it put other buildings to shame for even attempting something as ostentatious as, say, windows. It was situated between an all-night gymnasium and a cork mill. The walls had so much history in them that if they could have talked they would have been remarkable, as well as helping to drown out the sound next door of beefy men slamming body-building equipment about. (A sound which, incidentally, almost ruined my most memorable Thithterton performance: *Hot Ulysses Night* – my marriage of the Joyce masterpiece to the lyrics of the great Neil Diamond. When, as Stephen Daedalus, I crooned 'I am, I said', the sound of grunting and heaving next door killed all the dramatic tension. Still, it was a *tour de force* by anyone's standards, dampened ever so slightly by the fact that only a coachload of Rotarians from Hamilton showed up to see it.)

I first trod the Thithterton's boards in 1988. At the time I was an unknown, a bit player in the touring company of Sesame Street's *Equus*. I played the doctor who reattaches Kermit's retinas. After one particular performance, I was invited to the stately home of Anthony Truesdale – New Zealand's most revered actor – who achieved international fame as the voice of a cartoon muskrat. Anthony told me I had a great future in the theatre and I had no reason to doubt him, because he always carried around one of those plastic 8-balls with the weird prognostications that would float eerily to the surface – things like 'reply hazy, try again'. He was an original, Truesdale, and not without his eccentricities. For example, he eschewed cutlery at the dinner table, preferring instead to use a small wooden clothes peg to grasp his food. A tireless prankster, he thought nothing of lifting a grape from his plate, balancing it gently on his thumb, then thrusting it brutally into my eye socket. 'There's your Equus!' he would cackle, then suddenly go pensive, staring for hours into his 8-ball: a real cad, that man. He gave up the acting profession several years ago to pursue prison incarceration.

The dressing room was hearty and cosy, presided over by a matronly German woman named Matilde, who later turned out to be a man, and after that a woman again, and then something kind of in between – a cyborg maybe. Matilde pressed our costumes and made us tea. Sometimes, when we got her all liquored up, she would speak wistfully of her dream, which was to play professional hockey. She was married to one of the weightlifters from next door, a mountain of a man named Tito, but a gentle man really. Tito loved the theatre and would attend every Thithterton performance, clapping like a seal at all the great lines, then inexplicably demanding a shrimp treat as a reward. Sometimes Matilde would strap Tito to her back, weights and all, and she would pad around the dressing room minding her backstage duties whilst Tito dangled from her deltoids, doing his lovely ab crunches. They were a vibrant couple and I miss them.

There was a smaller stage directly beneath the main stage, a sort of launching pad for try-outs and experimental stuff, the kind of plays that are happy to have only thirty or so people in the audience. That's where I saw Faye Dunaway in *Sunset Boulevard*. The smaller theatre was hard to reach. One had to go down a flight of stairs, past the tech room, wind around a corridor, then cross an eight-lane superhighway with giant articulated lorries whizzing by in both directions. That's Auckland city planning for you!

Actually, an easier way to reach the stage was to simply fall through the rotting floorboards of the main stage above, which is exactly what happened to me on my last appearance there and goes a long way towards explaining how I ended up in the cast of an all-gay male musical called *Oklahomo!* Ah well, that's show biz.

men

MALE, 43, DOESN'T smoke, doesn't drink. Into fitness regime. I like classical music, especially Wagner's *Ring Cycle*, Tom Clancy novels, and pork chops. I'm stalwart and dependable. Seeking independent, free-spirited female who knows her own mind. Mustn't smoke or drink. Must be fit and into classical music, especially Wagner's *Ring Cycle*, Tom Clancy novels and cook a mean pork chop. Also must be stalwart and dependable. My name's Ed. Box 3119-B

Gentleman, 35, seeks female companion for quiet evenings of Scrabble, Monopoly, Whist or Cribbage. I'm straightforward and not into playing games. Box 4117

Male, 49, wants to know about the mystery dance. Why won't someone tell me about the mystery dance? I've tried and I've tried and I'm still mystified. I can't do it anymore and I'm not satisfied. Contact E. Costello. Box 5664

If you're tall, single and female you can put your shoes under my bed anytime. Write to Box 5998-G. Please specify shoe size.

Gay man, 43, seeks other gay men for bondage, humiliation, degradation, S&M, nipple-piercing, golden showers. Must be non-smoker. Box 533

Slugs are eating my chrysanthemums. Churchill was a tyrant. I'm itchy and mildly hirsute, allergic to mayonnaise. RU the 1 4 Me? Contact 657

Lifelong prisoner seeking good-hearted woman willing to oversee my faults. Must have sense of adventure and willingness to travel to remote exotic places. Box 1212. Also must own helicopter.

Hi, everyone! I'm a good-looking male, 30, who's not afraid to give of myself and nurture a relationship. I know the value of adventure, excitement, passion and romance – but more importantly I know that love is really about intimacy and understanding. I'm confident, flexible, hopelessly romantic, financially secure and guess what – DON'T NEED YOU!! THAT'S RIGHT, I'VE GOT IT WAY TOO TOGETHER. NO ONE, AND I MEAN NO ONE, GETS A PIECE OF ME!! STARE ALL YOU WANT, LADIES, IT AIN'T FOR SALE!! Box 987-C

SWM, 25, GSOH, PH.D MBA, RAC into TM, TA, AA, REM, M&Ms, needs TLC PDQ. ISO someone who understands me. Box 432

Hey, I'm trisexual. I'll 'try' anything!! Latex bubble wrapping, French, Greek, Tasmanian, Spanish

Inquisition, here comes the Monkees, Finnish Sumatran, 'Sink the Bismarck', jelly donuts, drilling for cobalt, frogs on the lily pad, Woolworth's Special, chicken dancing on a hot plate, cool nights in a big vat of barbeque sauce. Box 5643. No timewasters, please.

I'm tall, athletic and look like Gary Lineker. Address all correspondence to: Gary Lineker Box 453

Adventurous Male in search of someone who knows where they're going in life. Who is loyal and willing to shoulder their burden. Who likes the outdoors. All interested women or sherpas please contact box 675-A.

I've tried loving someone with all my heart and it hasn't worked. Is there anyone out there who might want to be loved with, say, all of my foot? Or perhaps all of my meniscus? I've got a lotta lovin' to give! Box 3215

new american west II

Glasgow, Montana.

Well, I finally made it. I've always wanted to come here, to see the Rocky Mountain's spiritual sister of that great Scottish city.

I'm fascinated by American towns that take their names from great European cities: Berlin, Ohio. London, Kentucky. Madrid, Missouri. John O'Groats, Arizona. (Actually that last one isn't a town at all, just some guy whose name I saw in a phone directory.) I like to visit these places to see if they've made any attempt to acknowledge their namesakes. On the outskirts of Glasgow, a billboard featured a Scottish terrier wearing a kilt and tam. It was the only vestige of Scotland I would find.

Glasgow sits on a high dusty ridge above the Missouri river, its buildings tilted in all directions like David Bowie's teeth. It's a railroad town, a greasy link on the route from Minneapolis to Seattle, full of hardscrabble men in baseball caps and women with gigantic jiggly butts that look like someone tried to cram a waterbed into a pair of wranglers.

In his book *Notes From a Small Island* Bill Bryson writes, hilariously, about trying to order a drink from an incoherent Glasgow pub landlord. In Montana it was the opposite. *They* couldn't understand *me*.

'What kinds of beer do you have?' I asked the barmaid at The Stockman's Bar.

'Bottled,' she replied.

'What brands?'

'Hun'h?'

'What are the *names* on the *labels* of beers you serve?'

'Uh, you'll have to come back and ask the owner. He's here in the daytime.'

A couple of hops technologists at the end of the bar attempted to answer me.

'Butt, Milk Lobe, Butt Light, Milk Lobe Light,' they said, by way of small-town hospitality. No one talked to me after that so I grabbed a copy of the *Glasgow Courier* and perused the sheriff's report page. *'A man called to report a calf on the middle of Highway 2.' 'A fight was reported at the palace bar. Sheriff's Deputies responded and broke it up.' 'A fight was reported at a house on East 5th St. It was a continuation of the fight at the Palace Bar.' 'A suspicious-looking man was asking Beer brands at The Stockman's.'*

Wow, does news travel fast here!

I spent the night at the Cambridge Motel, a place so frightening the Gideon's people won't even deliver Bibles there. All night long, trains rattled through town, cicadas shrieked and the couple in the next room were, as far as

I could tell, dressing up in suits of armour and jumping up and down on their bed.

In the morning, sleepless and testy, I wandered over to Johnnie's Café for coffee. It was already 90 degrees and the town was humming. (Later I realised the hum was coming from a power generating station down by the river.) I was searching intently for some trace of Scottishness, anything remotely linking the town to its big brother, but it just didn't exist. I tried some desperate leaps of the imagination: a railroad worker lugged a railroad tie like a caber. Yeah! An old truck tyre sticking out of a squalid pond could have been the Loch Ness Monster. Woohoo!

It was useless.

I walked over to the courthouse and asked a lady at the Glasgow Visitors' Bureau how the town had come by its name.

'Lots of Irish came over to work in the Butte Copper Mines,' she gallantly informed me. 'I guess some of 'em settled here.'

I got in my car and left Glasgow as quickly as possible. There was a supermarket on the outskirts of town and I stopped to buy some snacks for the long drive to North Dakota. On one of the shelves there was an assortment of snacks made by a company called Pepperidge Farms. Each cookie had an exotic name: Milano, Geneva, Bordeaux, Zurich. I wondered if most Americans, self-absorbed and culturally comatose, possessed any geographical awareness of what they were stuffing into their pie-holes.

North Dakota was better. Its German and Scandinavian heritage was proudly evident. There were restaurants advertising Lutefisk dinners. Bismarck was having its 'German Days'. I was starting to feel a faint rekindling of hope. Maybe, in this remote northern enclave, people

199

still had some inkling of their roots. I stopped off at the Peace Gardens – a memorial straddling the US–Canadian border commemorating 'Lasting Peace between America and Canada', as if there had ever been a problem. (Show me a garden commemorating Peace between America and, say, Iraq and I'll be impressed.)

America is like a beauty contestant. It's gorgeous, until it opens its mouth. And it's big on World Peace. If it doesn't know its roots, it just invents them. And there's always a surprise around the bend. In fact, according to my map, I should be pulling into Edinburg, North Dakota, any second now. Apparently it's predominately German.

parallel phenomena

NEWS ITEM: STEVE FOSSETT TO
LAUNCH HIMSELF IN SOLO
ROUND-THE-WORLD ATTEMPT

DECEMBER 12 2002 (*Reuters*) Millionaire Adventurer Steve Fossett announced today he will attempt, for the sixth time, to fly solo around the world. Looking tanned and confident, and sporting a substantial girth, Fossett said that this time he would not be using a balloon, but would float himself.

'I think my ego is now substantially inflated enough to forego the use of a balloon or any other aviation device,' said Fossett. 'Last month I climbed both Everest and K2 and competed in three Iron Man Triathlons. I also brokered several takeover deals through my Marathon Securities Inc., which netted me a cool couple of billion. There's no point in me being humble about this. I've always felt the need to prove that I would have been an astonishing individual capable of inhuman feats no matter what century I had lived in. That's why I'm a balloonist. Or rather at this point, a balloon.'

Fossett will try to achieve the goal that has fallen heart-breakingly short for him five times previously, most recently when weather conditions forced him to crash-land his craft in a mustard field in India.

'That won't happen this time,' said Fossett. 'If I start to deflate, I can merely remind myself of my recent dog-mushing trek across Antarctica, or my successful around-the-world voyage in an inflatable dinghy. That should pump me back up.'

Fossett will launch from Busch Stadium in St Louis, most likely in January of next year, when winter winds provide the best trajectory. He will probably choose a northern course, which would take him over the Atlantic Ocean, the English Channel ('which I have successfully crossed by backstroke four times'), Scandinavia ('my favourite country'), Russia, then toward Japan and finally over the Pacific Ocean.

In flight, Fossett will sleep sparingly. 'I prefer to stay awake and think about myself and all my accomplishments,' he said.

NEWS ITEM: LOCAL MAN MYSTERIOUSLY FLOATS AWAY

December 12 2002 (*Wheeling, W. Virginia Chronicle*) A local resident has been reported missing by his wife after he inexplicably floated off into the atmosphere. Dave Butterworth, 37, an unemployed oil-change technician and Wheeling native, apparently lifted off from his front porch yesterday afternoon and 'headed out over the city, towards Pennsylvania, thataway,' according to reports from his distraught wife, Bunny. She admitted the couple had been fighting prior to the incident.

'Bills. It was about bills,' Mrs Butterworth was reported as saying. 'We've had some money problems lately, but I don't see why he had to leave me holding the bag. The rat bastard.'

A check of Mr Butterworth's credit status by the city comptroller revealed Butterworth owed over $20,000 to Citibank Visa, as well as a plethora of unpaid bills from various local establishments. Also $8,000 in unpaid parking tickets.

Although police are at a loss to explain Butterworth's admittedly odd disappearance, Ed Huckert, a credit-recovery specialist for Consolidated Debt Associates Inc., has his own theory.

'I think there's no question that Dave has undergone what we call an "out-of-money" experience,' explained Huckert. 'When you owe as much money as Dave, it becomes downright spiritual. The deeper a man gets into debt the more it eats away at his insides. Eventually you're just a shell of a man. At that point all them hot-air excuses and lofty promises you've been blowing at credit managers like us, the "if-I-cans" and when "I-get-its" . . . well, they start to back up on ya . . . This creates an optimum airborne condition. You brung it on yerself, all's I got to say about it.'

Mr Huckert admitted that recently, in an attempt to get Butterworth to pay up, he had been 'trying to light a fire under his ass. I guess that's what set him aloft. My guess is he's headed for Fiji,' added Huckert. 'I wouldn't put it past that deadbeat to try and cross the International Dateline just to get a day's jump of his bills. I read about that once in a *Merman* comic book.'

bad reviews follow me wherever i go

Wellington, New Zealand

W HAT CAN YOU say about a country where 60% of all police responses fall under the classification: Noisy Party. Not 'prowlers', not 'attempted breaking and entering', not 'man making percussion instrument from the rib cage of strangulation victim'. Nope. Noisy Party. People having too good a time. Generally I'm sceptical of people who put too much emphasis on recreation, but there's no way you can't like Kiwis. They're fairly harmless and eager to please and they can't help it if they're the most boring people on the face of the planet and speak in a tonic register that sounds like a buzzsaw hitting a rusty nail.

Kiwis have willingly and graciously melded an astounding diaspora of various pacific cultures within their tiny space. They have clean roads, spectacular landscapes and eight million varieties of coffee, all of which sound like railroad hoboes from the thirties: Flat White, Long Black, Slim Mocha. Ordering coffee in New Zealand is like picking out interior paint. They're deceptively potent as well. Sinisterly hiding beneath its milky veil, the Flat White is actually a concentrated nuclear frisson of caffeinated plutonium which, when ingested, transforms you into a dynamo of misguided ambition. I drank three cups in an hour and have since decided to become a professional drummer.

Which would probably be a better career choice than the one I am currently pursuing. Until I arrived in New Zealand, I *thought* I was a comedian. This tiny island nation has collectively decided otherwise. As far as I'm concerned, they have it in for me. I have a stonking great show to tour and it's not my fault if the audience doesn't get it.

When I first came up with the idea of *Rich Hall on Ice* people said, 'Rich, it's crazy. Nobody wants to see standup on ice skates.' But my mind was made up. I spent an entire year honing my skating techniques, practising adagio movements, writing new material, and then I get to the Wellington Civic Arts Theatre and, hey, *there's no rink!* It was specified in my contract! Doesn't anybody read these things?

So now I'm clopping out on to the wooden floorboards of the stage every night in ice skates and, admittedly, it must be somewhat baffling to the audience. Also, the sequinned unitard is damned scratchy under those hot lights. Then there's the chorus of 'Nice Package!' cat calls coming from the drunken yobbos in the back row, but it's not a compliment, not with that sandpaper accent, no thank you. This is the kind of shit I have to put up with for being a pioneer.

Some people have been whingeing about the show's length, which clocks in at just under six hours. Goddammit, it's a lean, mean six hours! There's not an ounce of gristle in that six hours! The show starts at midnight, it's over at sun-up. That's a lot of bang for the buck if you ask me.

Plus, my show has incisive political content. I detest these comics who claim to be 'political' and then trot out a few lame-o one-liners about how dumb George Bush is. That's not political! Me, I have something to say and I say it. For example, around four a.m. I launch into a blistering chunk about the duplicity of Burmese Freedom Fighters – how their ideologies belie their romantic notion of the post-socialist agenda. 'Everyone knows they're just trying to take over the lucrative Asian rattan trade,' I say – and I really use my growly delivery to good effect there. *Meanwhile*, the whole time I'm pointing this out, I'm executing a deft series of complicated pirouettes – well, as deft as one can possibly be on lumpy floorboards. What do I get from the audience? Fish-faced yawns! Folks, it's comedy! Howsabout lettin' your hair down for a change?

The reviews haven't helped. Only one newspaper, the *Wellington News*, covered the show, and I'm pretty sure the person they sent was an erstwhile food critic:

> Leave it to an American to serve up a bland and tasteless serving of underdone tripe! Rich Hall's comedy casserole *Rich Hall on Ice* came in a dish that could best be described as chafing. Half-baked premises and a curdled delivery left a bitter after-taste in this critic's mouth.

207

Ouch. Like I said, what do they know? The bane of an artist is never truly to be understood.

Auckland

Desolate on a Sunday noon. A frigate bird slinks across an empty street, knowing he's got the place to himself. Supposedly there are humans ensconced in these high-rise buildings surrounding me, which have all the architectural appeal of Shane MacGowan's teeth. In fact, the uniform building code for Auckland seems to adhere to something Mondrian would have come up with were he colour-blind and had been supplied with an Etch-a-Sketch and a fifth of Jack Daniels. The harbour is beautiful. The geography is appealing. But the buildings are just stout and grey, random as gravestones.

Aucklanders pride themselves on their outdoor zest. Within its fifty-mile radius, one has access to sailing, sport-fishing, scuba-diving, spelunking, mountain climbing, geyser watching, volcano observing and, of course, hurling drunken taunts at large Samoans on the city streets late at night. Kiwis proudly boast there 'are no animals in New Zealand that can kill you'. Consequently, Kiwis can attribute their healthy rate of deaths each year to sailing, sport-fishing, volcano observing, Samoan teasing and so on. Presumably, they're all out killing themselves in the great outdoors because there's sure as hell nothing going on in these streets.

I ambled over towards Ponsonby Road, pretending to myself I was Charlton Heston in *The Omega Man*. I finally found a restaurant open. It served Mexican/Malaysian food. I was thinking there must be some kind of metaphysical Grand Canyon that would prevent these

208

two cultures from ever meeting on the same plate, when the affable lone waiter came over to take my order then retreated to the kitchen to work up his hip/hop Mexi-Malay miracle concoction. To this day I'm not sure what I ate. I think it was a Roti Burrito.

Afterwards, I walked down to Marsden Wharf to contemplate the spot where, in 1985, Greenpeace's eco-dinghy the *Rainbow Warrior* was sunk by French 'agents', allegedly for being nettlesome. A plaque showed a photo of the boat and it was tiny, a whale snack. Whales are what the *Rainbow Warrior* was trying to save. I love whales as much as the next person. I think about them at least fourteen seconds a year. But I don't see how a handful of crusty pot-addled water yahoos in a rusty squeak toy like the *Warrior* ever expected to make much of a dent towards their survival. And in fact they didn't. The plaque marks the spot where the Green Revolution suffered its Greatest Naval Loss. A hippie died.

What Auckland does have going for it is a vigorous dose of good old multiculturalism – and its attendant handmaiden, racial tension. Unlike the Australians, who get a little jittery at the mere mention of the M word, Kiwis have thoughtfully attempted to integrate Maoris and Pacific Islanders into their society. In other words they haven't slaughtered them the way the Aussies did. And on Saturday nights, when the town actually *does* show a pulse, Queen Street is abuzz with a lusty gumbo of Maoris, Fijians, Samoans, Tongans, Cook Islanders and other transplants from the Malaria Belt. There is also a festering melange of barking drunks, cloying uni students, stinky backpackers and Bogans. (Characteristically, Bogans wear black jeans, drive old cars, drink lots of beer and possess limited conversational skills. In Britain the equivalent word is 'Poet'.)

The primary result of this valiant social experiment – mixing cultures, alcohol and nightlife – is, as I'm sure you've guessed, lots of fistfights. I counted at least a dozen on my Saturday night in Auckland. One, involving Samoans, Bogans and their respective girlfriends, took on the magnitude of a WWF Texas Death Match. Amazingly, to me, no handguns were produced, even though New Zealand has the third highest concentration (per capita) of handguns in the world. (Right behind the US and, for some strange reason, Finland. This astounds me. I've never once read a headline proclaiming 'Armed Finn in Crazed Lapland Hostage Drama'. Maybe they're all being used as reindeer tranquillisers.)

Anyway, by Sunday morning, the hooha was well over, and Auckland was back to its desultory, lifeless pace. I sat for hours and watched the frigate birds, who sat for hours and watched me. None of the animals can kill you. But the boredom can.

After the critical drubbing I'd received in Wellington, I decided to rewrite my show for the Auckland audience. Witnessing, at Marsden Wharf, what happens when you try to get too political in New Zealand, I thought I might go for more of a dramatic slant. I retitled my show *FDR in Yalta* and, zipping around stage in a wheelchair, delivered a loose interpretation of Franklin Delano Roosevelt's historic postwar meeting with Winston Churchill and Joseph Stalin. Acknowledging Aucklanders' penchant for active sports, I worked in a subplot where the three world leaders engage in a cut-throat ping pong match to decide Berlin's fate. Naturally, this involved the need for two other actors. Casting was a bit of a problem. Not just *anyone* can play ping pong and recite lengthy passages of historical dialogue at the same time, and several critics openly questioned why both Stalin *and* Churchill were Chinese. Again, the reviews were beyond dismal. Not only did my bold *tour de force* garner *no* stars, the critics actually *subtracted* stars from several other productions in town at the time, thus creating a sort of theatrical black hole for me to crawl out of. I had to give money back to my producers and take over the theatre's mortgage payments. Suffice it to say, I won't be coming back to this town.

Christchurch

Arriving here as a guest of the Christchurch International Performing Arts Festival, I find myself relegated to a small performance space called the Carrot Exchange, notable for its odd geometric configuration. As far as I can tell, the room is nine sided, with the seating arranged like a thwarted prototype of Stonehenge. The stage, craftily comprised of plastic milk crates, sits in one corner, whilst the seats (benches actually) face an entirely different direction altogether, thus requiring the audience twist their necks in an obscenely chiropractic angle to view my antics. It occurred to me that perhaps the attendee is supposed to *straddle* the bench, which would give me the vague sensation of performing to a galley of Viking ship rowers. Show business is an altogether different thing down here, but people with strong peripheral vision are digging my new show.

Flying down to the South Island, I'd pulled out the Air New Zealand in-flight magazine to have a look at the map in the back. The shapes of countries always fascinate me, far more than their politics or culture, which are always in flux. Shapes never change. Everyone knows, for example, that Italy resembles a boot, but look closely and you'll notice that the Philippines resembles a scorpion crawling amongst the remains of a shattered disco ball. Laos is a dead ringer for Lisa Simpson. Check it out if you don't believe me. And if you study Sulawesi (off Borneo) you'll agree that it is that weird griffin-looking monster on the tail end of a British pound coin.

Here's another thing. Maps of the world generally shade each country in pink, green, amber, what-have-you, for contrast and definition. I noticed on the plane that New Zealand was green, which makes perfect sense, because New Zealand *is* green. But so is Great Britain. So how come Great Britain was urine yellow on the map? Also, Australia, the US, Zaire and Brazil were pink. A few days later, passing an office supply shop in Christchurch, I saw a map in the window and noted that, again, the countries were the same colours as in the in-flight magazine.

It occurred to me that somewhere (and I'm guessing Brussels) there is a governing board for coordinated universal map shading, and within that board is a guy whose job it is to decide what colour a country gets to be, *and he gets paid to do it*. Oh how he must wallow in his pointless authority, reducing entire nations to an emasculating pink, or pissing on them with unabashed glee, until they're stained a uniform yellow.

I only point this out because everyone seems to be alarmed by the bureaucratic miasma that pervades our day-to-day lives and I, for one, champion individuality and I can't believe we live under an oppressive code that tells us what colour we have to be.

Thus by the time I hit the makeshift stage of the Christchurch Carrot Exchange I was infused with a passionate and righteous zeal and delivered a sizzling unscripted two-hour diatribe called *Pink Like Me*. You can't, I fervently implored, judge a country by its colour anymore than you can an individual. I wish I could say the audience was enraptured. But I can't even say they went so far as to even just stare at me. Given the seating arrangement, they kind of observed me, warily, from the corners of their eyes.

Still, I don't think it was fair of the *Christchurch Herald* to print the review of my show in the obituaries section:

DEATHS: Hall, Rich (on stage) at the Carrot Exchange. We wish to console all those who attended Mr Hall's performance and sat with him during his protracted and debilitating decline. His valiant fight to almost be funny was an inspiration to us all.

Dunedin

I feel Edinburgh should be warned. It has a twin city, a shadow city, a cheap impostor trying to pass itself off as the 'Edinburgh of the Southern Hemisphere'. As comparisons go, it almost works, provided you're resilient with your imagination. Edinburgh has Robert Burns. Dunedin has Robbie Burns' All-Nite Liquor Warehouse. Edinburgh sits near a volcanic plug. Dunedin sits near an *active volcano*. On the inside cover of Dunedin's Yellow Pages are instructions on 'What To Do in the Event of an Eruption'. Step number three is 'cover your head'. Apparently volcanoes are Muslim.

The town itself, situated near the bottom of the South Island, is perpendicular to Edinburgh. Were you to flatten the earth into a billiards table, they would be corresponding corner pockets. It came into existence in the mid-1800s, primarily as the epicentre of a gold rush. So it has retained all the solid values that come from a lineage of prospectors, get-rich-quick schemers, scammers and vagrants. The story related to me by a trustworthy local historian – well, a taxi driver actually – is that townsfolk wanted a Scottish name for their boomtown but were torn between Edinburgh and – I'm not making this up – Dundee. Hence, Dunedin . . . glorious compromise.

In the middle of town sits a miniature replica of Edinburgh's Scott Memorial which, due to its reduced scale, resembles either a Victorian monkey jungle or the skeletal remains of a Ku Klux Klansman. That's the Edinburgh concession. The Dundee concession is, quite naturally, Perpetual Gloom. The people of Dunedin sit around hunkering from the cold, eating soup and wondering why no other city has ever located itself within view of Antarctica.

I came down here to play The Regent's Theatre, which squats in the centre of town on a plaza called the Octagon, thus creating a peripheral traffic nightmare of motorists making endless right turns in order to go around in a circle. Amazingly, about seven hundred people managed to find their way to my new show, *Smoke On the Water*, a faithful recreation of the famous Deep Purple song about a boat ablaze on a Swiss lake. (The entire set and props were ingeniously confined to the contents of a tropical fish aquarium.) Seven hundred people would be considered an impressive turnout were it not for the fact that the Regent seats roughly 70,000. It is without a doubt the biggest theatre I've ever been in. Before it was a theatre it was, I believe, an Olympic stadium, and before that, a Lost City. The seven hundred people looked like capers floating in a swimming pool. Whatever laughs I cadged won't actually hit the stage until next June.

Since I was the biggest thing to hit Dunedin since Prospector Pete's 1861 Whistling Goldmine Canary revue, my photo was prominently splashed across half the front page of the *Otago Daily Times* – Dunedin's feeble link to the outside world. The photographer used an unflattering fish-eye lens, no doubt for comical effect, so Dunedin's citizens were forewarned by a queasy panorama of a gigantic misshapen face, promising them a forthcoming evening of mirth and mayhem. All day long I had to walk around and confront my own visage bulging – Tex Avery like – from every newsstand in town. When I actually walked out on stage that night, I think people were collectively relieved to see I wasn't an Amazon Trout. At least the *Otago Daily Times* review was forgiving:

Mr Hall was wise not to make cheap cracks about our filthy weather.

Thus my tour of this murky paradise ended on an uplifting note.

Returning to Britain's pee-stained shores, I couldn't help but look back on my trip with a forgiving fondness. New Zealand is the gentlest country I've ever been to. So what if they killed a hippie? So what if they have accents that sound gas-powered? You have to admit there's something comforting about knowing a place still exists where if you're a cop responding to an emergency call, there's a better than 50/50 chance that the most life-threatening tactic you'll have to employ is saying, 'Hey! turn that thing down!'

Gaudi sympathised with him. It's possible the two were drinking at the time.

Both architects had experimented with edible edifices before. Several years earlier, Gaudi had published plans for a park enclosure constructed entirely of marzipan, while Mackintosh had actually built a tiny nativity scene from confectioner's sugar, which featured as its centre-piece a shortbread manger. The Church of Scotland quickly condemned it. Gaudi's plan was ridiculed by peers, who believed marzipan to be too sticky to use as building material. Neither man was daunted. Nor were they strangers to gingerbread. Both had sampled it and found it delightful.

The idea was to unveil their competing houses at the 1888 Worlds Fair in Barcelona. Gaudi set about baking at once. He was beset, almost from the start, by design problems. 'The architect is a man who synthesises but does not yet possess the wisdom and infinite intuition of the angels, who alone are capable of building without planning ahead,' he once remarked. He was a religious man but it would be safe to say he was scared to death of death, or rather of the afterlife. He was certain angels had no regard for spatial economy and feared heaven was just a sprawling omelette of rampant, slapdash architec-ture, much like Birmingham. He hated angles, a word he often confused with 'angels' (Gaudi was dyslexic). This is echoed in his work, which relies so much on serpen-tine shapes, nautilas spirals and skeletal-bone-like supports. He wanted the gingerbread house to *resemble a house*, but feared that, out of context, it might be viewed as nothing more than an amorphous loaf. Thus he wres-tled with just how the gingerbread house should look.

Mackintosh, on the other hand, was well suited to the task. His design was more or less inspired by the baking of Aubrey Beardsley, who had come up with a rudimentary gingerbread man several years before. Using Beardsley's basic recipe – which called for pre-heating the oven to 350°F, then combining flour, sugar and ground ginger – Mackintosh came up with the inspired idea of adding blackstrap molasses, which gave the mixture a burnished, oaken complexion, the same signature colour that runs prominently in his highback chairs and other furniture. He worked meticulously, using right triangles and a mitre box, and the house – completed over a period of eighteen months – came out a perfect integration of design, function and taste. Unfortunately, one of his students ate it by accident. His second attempt, though hastily constructed, was a more austere, but nonetheless breathtaking creation. It featured meringue latticework. That same inspired ornamentation today adorns the library of the Glasgow School of Art.

Whereas Mackintosh could rely on his wife, Virginia, to help oversee the baking, Gaudi – a lifelong bachelor – found himself quite alone and exasperated. As the Worlds Fair deadline approached, he sank into a deep funk of depression, listlessness and indecision. He experimented with corn syrup, sugarbeets, fructose, honey, Turkish taffy and, briefly, linoleum. Nothing seemed to work. His attempts at baking came out a molten lumpen mess. He refused to use mixing bowls or spoons, believing them to be too regimented. Instead he designed his own mixing implements, typically nonlinear and slightly misshapen. Take a look at that spatula in your kitchen drawer. You have Gaudi to thank for that.

The concoction that Gaudi finally unveiled on the opening night of the Worlds Fair was beyond description. It did not resemble a house as much as a cathedral of crust: rambling out of control, devoid of proportion.

get out of bed

NAOMI CAMPBELL IS retiring. I can't believe I had to read it in the papers. Surely she must've considered calling me. We go back a long way, Naomi and I. There was never anything between us, if that's what you're thinking. Not emotionally anyway. It was just pure, high-octane sex, and frankly that's all I could really ever offer her. Naomi is far too intimidating a woman for me to handle – beyond raw animal sex.

Oh sure, she wanted me to be all things to her: lover, confidant, spiritual pillar, intellectual sparring partner, business advisor, muse, bedroom acrobat . . . I couldn't be there for her, not completely. She claims I broke her heart. I suppose I did. But I'm here to tell you there's a world of difference between the Naomi Campbell you imagine and the Naomi Campbell *I've* come to know. Your idea of Naomi, I would guess, is 'stunning world-famous fashion model who says she can't take the stress of strolling up and down the catwalk anymore'. Or, perhaps, 'self-inflated bag of ribs who allows hyperactive designer twits to hang their hysterical creations on to her perpetually starved frame'. Well you would, in a limited capacity, be correct, sir. But Naomi is much more than a rickety clothes peg.

The truth is, Naomi is so overstretched from her tireless schedule of hostage negotiating, foreign-policy making, economic advising, scientific pursuit and general ambassadorial globe-trotting that she barely has time to exhibit Thierry Mugler's latest creation of frocks made from bits of cork and carpet samples.

The recent events leading up to her retirement announcement due to 'stress', should give a pronounced indication of the kind of duress poor Naomi has had to endure:

Feb 1: The disarmament agreement in Northern Ireland is faltering. Realising that an impasse has been reached with Sinn Fein on the decommissioning of weapons, Tony Blair interrupts Naomi in the middle of her Milan Preview of Floppy Summer Hats and begs her to serve as an intermediary. After some furious reshuffling, whereby US Senator George Mitchell agrees to replace her on the catwalk, Naomi immediately jets to Belfast and – after a quick nap – lends her finely honed voice of equanimity to an escalating crisis. She cooly advises the IRA to produce some 'Good Faith Semtex', as a gesture of conciliation. This is exactly what the IRA needs: an opportunity to propitiate without losing face. What is lost, however, in the tense hours of negotiation, is sleep, valuable sleep. Naomi gets only ten of the thirteen hours she requires to maintain her mental well-being, elasticity and 'white' energy.

Feb 2: Naomi's renowned composure is further strained by an argument with the editor-in-chief of *Scientific American* magazine. Ms Campbell, whose work in nuclear physics single-handedly unearthed the existence of a new and undiscovered atomic particle several years ago (called the *naoman*), is at odds with the editor over whether her discovery is, in fact, a *specific* particle or a *rogue* particle. The truculent editor claims Ms Campbell's gamma ray tests – in which the emissions of the *naoman* are measured in a bubble chamber at spin state – are not classifiable in terms of their existence. Ms Campbell fiercely argues that they do 'exist' – if for only a hundredth of a billion of a second – and thereby constitute matter. The editor stands by his argument. What is at stake is not only Naomi's credibility in the physics community, but the front cover of March's *Scientific American*.

Defiantly, Naomi proves her case by recreating the event using a makeshift supercollider improvised from a blowdrier and an all-purpose juicer. Though she emphatically proves her argument, the juicer gets mucked up and she has to forego her daily Smoothie. Still, what a gal! Now hungry and irritable, Naomi's rock solid constitution is starting to show signs of wear. Ms Campbell flies to Paris by Concorde. The complimentary cosmetics travel kit is not up to her standards. Arriving in Paris, she goes straight to bed. Things are unravelling dangerously.

Feb 3: Naomi's sharklike business acumen is called into question by her own agents. Proclaiming that she 'doesn't get out of bed for less than $500,000', her agents propose a fee-schedule based on incentives. To wit:

Getting out of bed $500,000
Getting out of bed and padding to the kitchen
for a glass of water $750,000
Getting out of bed naked $1,000,000

Naomi is justifiably incensed that someone else would try to put a price on her talents. She sulks off and spends the rest of the day in bed.

Feb 4: Naomi throttles her assistant for arguing against the merits of the plummeting Euro. In a hastily assembled press conference, she announces she can no longer handle the stress of runway modelling *and* monitor an ongoing European economic crisis. Decisions such as whether to binge/purge *before* or *after* a fitting are tormenting her beyond relief. She claims the gruelling combination of walking and turning is taking its toll on her psyche. She states that she will 'walk' but no longer 'turn' for future fashion events, and demands runways stretching for 'at least a mile'.

Feb 5: A major fashion critic publicly states that Naomi has become 'petulant, tyrannical and unbearable'. Shattered, Naomi announces her retirement, then goes back to bed.

Feb 6: Naomi stays in bed.

Feb 7: Naomi stays in bed

Feb 8: Naomi stays in bed.

C'mon, Naomi, my little cupcake glamourpuss. Don't be so hard on yourself. You're too strong a woman to let a little bit of bad press get you down. Maybe you just need consolation and physical comfort. This is me talking. Call me. If you're home in bed, call me, pick up the phone and call me. Call me, call me, call me, call me, call me.

Incidentally, what does that cost?

squirrel apologies

I GOT A wart on my hand. It first appeared about three months ago as an insignificant bump, then grew at such an alarming rate I thought maybe I was going to be consumed. No one seemed to be able to explain it to me, other than, 'It's a virus. Who knows?'

Somebody must know. How can we put atoms on an electron raceway but not know where warts come from? Medicine may have bigger fish to fry but me, I have to keep my hands in my pockets every moment I'm in public like some bumpkin.

Don't tell me it's frogs. I haven't handled a frog in years. But that just goes to show you how something like warts brings out the crackpot in normally sensible people. My friend Lisa told me to rub raw meat on it.

'What kind of raw meat,' I asked.

'A pork chop,' she said.

I went out and bought a pork chop, a healthy looking one too. While I was frottaging my hand with a pink marbled slab of perfectly good pork, I thought to myself, it's 2002 and I'm rubbing myself with meat. Slightly disconcerting.

The wart kept growing.

'You need to go to a graveyard under a full moon and pour witch hazel over it,' said my otherwise perfectly rational stepsister, a Princeton graduate who works for a genetic engineering firm in North Carolina.

'I can't remotely believe that's gonna work,' I said. I was calling her long distance.

'Worked for me twice,' she replied.

'If it worked, why did you have to do it twice?' I said.

'I don't know. They come back,' she answered, then hung up and went back to replicating DNA.

Lemme tell you, graveyards are pretty goddamned creepy even in the daytime. At night, with the full moon reflecting on those headstones, it was right out of a Hammer film. I probably would've freaked out had it not been for the reassuring presence of at least five other similarly afflicted wart-sufferers, all of us scudding amongst the tombstones, bottles of witch hazel concealed in bags, like graveyard winos. I'm sure by day these people were bankers, teachers, model citizens. Here, we were amateur warlocks. A discussion broke out as to whether it actually was a full moon above. Somebody pointed out we *might* be a night early.

'Look, there's a little chunk missing in the corner,' said a guy who I'm not sure, but I think may have been my dry cleaner.

We all argued over this for a good fifteen minutes. Then I dumped the witch hazel over my offending carbuncle and hot-footed it out of there.

The wart prospered: Friends kept offering up suggestions that belied their otherwise well-earned credibility.

'Moisten some cigarette tobacco and make a compress on the wart.'

'Tape a copper coin to the wart for three days.'

'Put on a tungsten bracelet and go swimming in the ocean. Backwards.'

'Ignore it and it will go away. Maybe.'

'Have a cat lick it, then hold the cat upside down and pray to St Francis of Assisi.'

'Here's what you gotta do. Grind up some betel nuts, rub that on them, then fly round trip to Vancouver, Canada.' Granted, that one came from my travel agent.

I bought something called Bazuka and applied it to the wart. By then two more had sprouted on the same hand. Within minutes the ointment turned a crusty white and now *everyone* noticed my hand. I looked like I'd punched a clown.

'What happened to your hand?' said my dry cleaner.

'*You know*,' I answered, eyeing him.

'What?'

'Never mind. Uh, warts.'

'Ugh. You tried a pork chop?'

My friend Karen Koren, who's Swedish, claimed her grandmother had a surefire remedy. '"Punch a black squirrel three times," she used to say.'

I spent a good five days looking for a black squirrel, to no avail. Eventually I settled for capturing a brown squirrel and spray-painting him black, but I couldn't bring myself to punch the little fella. We stared at each other for a while. He looked like he wanted an explanation. I let him go in the park.

Meanwhile the warts on my knuckles were starting to resemble aerial maps of Yellowstone National Park – red and craterish.

A lot of people – again, *normally reliable people* – said

I could just 'wish' the warts away. Is that so, I said. So how come you can't wish freckles away? Or birthmarks? Or George W. Bush? People who say things like this are just casting a safe bet, because eventually warts *do* go away, which makes them either benignly malignant or malignantly benign, I'm not sure which, but anyway, there's four medical words in a row with g-n in the middle of them, so there!

Back to the warts. They got bigger. So I decided to embrace the twenty-first century and seek proper treatment. I went to a doctor on Harley Street. Personally, I don't think it's very professional for a doctor who spends his day dealing with fissures, lesions, and other skin disfigurements to look at your hand and say, 'God, that's disgusting. I just had lunch!'

He informed me that if I wished to wait in the NHS queue, I could probably receive free treatment roughly by the time I was actually a walking volcano. *Or*, for £150, he could treat me right away.

He led me into a room full of sophisticated-looking equipment, sat me down beside a table, strapped on protective eyewear, a metal-plated chest protector and a pair of elbow length gloves. This was more like it, I thought. Why hadn't I put my faith in modern medicine to begin with? Then he walked over to a small cage in the corner of the room, pulled out a small black squirrel and started punching it.

A few weeks later I flew to New York City on business and figured that while I was there, I'd explore any American breakthroughs in wart technology. Cosmetic surgery in the US is way, way ahead of every other branch of medicine, and if you don't believe me, just look at Goldie Hawn. She's 107. I looked in the Manhattan

Yellow Pages under *Physicians* and there were twelve pages of ads for Dermatology/Skin Care specialists, each trying to outdo the other in wart sensationalism:

Warts? Lesions? Why suffer?
Dr Barton Foutz is here to help!
Don't delay. KILL THEM NOW!

Wow! Dr Foutz sounded downright mercenary. And from the accompanying photo, he looked like he walked the talk. So I called the number and, sure enough, he could see me that very afternoon.

Lemme just tell you something about health care in America. If your head was severed and lying in the middle of the road six feet away from your torso, the first thing the arriving paramedic would do would be to ask, 'Who's your HMO, pal?', jam a pencil in your teeth and guide your head through twenty pages of patient information forms. Then you would get treatment.

Which is what I did. It took almost twenty minutes to fill out the medical history exam. It took only three minutes for Dr Foutz to treat me.

He sat me down, held up my hand, examined the warts, bared his teeth in clear disgust and told me what he was going to do, *as* he was doing it.

'I'm gonna give you a smidgeon of Novocain,' he said and whoop-de-do, jabbed a glistening needle right into the pustules . . . 'slice 'em off with this razorblade' . . . zlit . . . 'freeze it with this liquid nitro' . . . flizzzzzzz!! . . . 'you haven't taken any aspirin lately, have you?'

'As a matter of fact, I have.'

'Oh. In that case, I'll just coagulate the blister with this electro-flocculator Roentgen administrator' . . . zzzzzzzzzzzt! . . . (Here he amassed most of the electricity in the building, funnelled it through a kind of metal pencil device and let fly with a fusillade of crackling, smoking electrical fireworks that lit my warts up like Vegas at night and made me dance an indoor watusi.) 'Take that, you sonofabitch!!' he seethed. I think he was talking to the warts.

Smoke was still coming off my knuckles as he slathered on about a pound of ointment then shoved me out into the anteroom to settle up with the nurse. I bled all over the cheque.

'I won't be seeing you back here!!' he brayed as I was leaving.

That was two weeks ago. The warts are gone, but now I have equally disgusting scabs the colour of sugar beets on my hand. Maybe I should have persevered with the folk remedies. Voodoo doesn't leave scars.

dear john response
(annotated)

Darling Rich,

I don't quite know how to say this, so I suppose I'll just come to the point. I think maybe we should call it quits. As much as I adore you and the times we've shared, I just don't feel I can spend my life with you. I need to be with someone who is less self-obsessed and . . . well, not such a control freak. Someone who doesn't flaunt their intelligence in front of my face all the time. Please understand this is not an easy thing for me to do. I shall miss you. You will always be in my heart.

> Best of luck,
> Patti

Patti.

Bitch. Whore. Faithless Slattern[1]. You've got some nerve calling me a control freak[2]. And self-obsessed?!!!³ If I'm so self-obsessed, then answer me this: WHO PAID FOR THE WEEKEND AT MT RUSHMORE??⁴ Jeeezus, I only went there because YOU WANTED TO GO!!!! Boy, talk about stabbing someone in the back⁵. I never saw this one coming. You can kiss my ass in Macy's window⁶. And give me back my inflatable Budweiser chair, midget-tits (sic).

    R.

SOURCE NOTES

(1) 'Slattern': a carelessly dressed and sloppy woman. Occasionally there is some reference to low manners or other negative characteristics. *Dictionary of Slang and Euphemism* (New York: NAL Penguin Books 1982)

(2) *See* Karen Finley '. . . usually the people who tell us to stop controlling others are the ones who are in control but want to appear to be free, easy and open. Getting people not to be in control [changes the power structure].' *Enough is Enough* (Toronto: Poseidon Press 1993)

(3) *See* Alexis de Tocqueville '. . . The affairs of daily life rarely involve concern for a larger community in such a way as to make the public and private merge in one's thoughts. It is merely that one is free to participate or not to participate . . . it is difficult to see himself as an integral part of something larger rather than merely an atom in a constantly changing continuum.' (New York: Simon & Schuster 1987)

(4) 'Thanks to the interstate highway system, it is now possible to travel across the country from coast to coast without seeing anything.' Charles Kuralt, *On the Road* (New York: Putnam 1985)

(5) 'Et tu Brutus?' William Shakespeare (*Julius Caesar*, various publications)

(6) Original source unknown. Macy's is a department store in New York City. Overheard on several occasions from my friend, Art Rumfelt. Used with kind permission.

ACKNOWLEDGMENTS

I clearly recognise that I could not have produced this letter, given my current distraught state of mind, without the help of the following people:

John Novotny (you the man, brother!!): who turned my helpless mess of a response letter into real pages, and even assisted in the layout and graphic design. Thanks for being there, bro.

My Parents (Doris and Burt): who taught me the value of a good education and loaned me the gas money so I could chauffeur my bitch-whore of a girlfriend to S. Dakota just to look at some stupid mountain.

Tom Petty and the Heartbreakers: '. . . you don't have to live like a refugee'. Man, those lyrics kept my head screwed on when I needed it most.

The Jack Daniels Corporation (Lynchburg, Tenn.).

Art Rumfelt: keep on sharpenin' those axes, dude.

Professor Langley (emeritus) Georgetown University, dept of English: who always said, 'Document everything!'

INDEX

235

ABOUT THE AUTHOR

Rich Hall is a man who feels flummoxed by love. In this break-through letter he examines, lucidly, the ever-widening gap in human relationships. He is currently single and enjoys reading and outdoor pursuits. His most recent project was a trip to Mt Rushmore, which has been described as 'a savage journey into the heart of the American Nightmare'.